INTERIOR DESIGN
STUDENT'S

Comprehensive Exam

INTERIOR DESIGN STUDENT'S

Comprehensive Exam

Lisa Godsey

Fairchild Books

New York

Executive Editor: Olga T. Kontzias
Senior Development Editor: Jennifer Crane
Associate Art Director: Erin Fitzsimmons
Production Director: Ginger Hillman
Senior Production Editor: Elizabeth Marotta
Assistant Acquisitions Editor: Amanda Breccia
Copyeditor: Progressive Information Technologies
Text Design: Dutton and Sherman
Compositor: Progressive Information Technologies

Library of Congress Catalog Card Number: 2009920357
ISBN: 978-1-56367-682-6
GST R 133004424
Printed in the United States of America
CH13, TP13

CONTENTS

INTRODUCTION

The qualifying exam for interior design professionals is the National Council for Interior Design Qualification (NCIDQ) exam. Students often express curiosity and dread about the exam, which is how many seasoned professionals feel as they plan their own study sessions and exam dates. The exercises contained in this collection are intended to simulate test-taking experiences similar to those found in the NCIDQ. Hopefully the exercises will be a fun challenge, since students working on these exercises don't have to worry about their career advancement hanging in the balance the way it does for professionals taking the exam. These exercises are intended to be an introduction to some of the content, scope, and pacing of the exam. They are not endorsed by NCIDQ, nor are they self testing exercises for professionals preparing for the exam. They are student exercises that imitate features of the exam, which help answer student questions about the exam experience.

This comprehensive collection of exercises covers topics similarly to those found in the NCIDQ, including space planning, business considerations, codes, advanced design planning, documentation, and so on. The exercises include a design portion and a multiple choice test portion. Both portions anticipate at least junior status and possibly senior status for successful completion, but it is possible to use the design portion as a space-planning exercise and present it with the topic of NCIDQ even earlier in the program.

This collection of exercises includes a multiple-choice test and four scenarios. This allows the exercises to be easily available to student groups year after year. The sheer number of questions will make it harder for students who have been through the exercise to pass specific information along to students who have yet to participate.

The four design scenarios will allow instructors to cycle through the alternate scenarios, making it more difficult for students to get advance word of the scenario from the previous years' students. Instructors can also run multiple scenarios at the same time so distribution can be randomized among students taking the test in cramped conditions, where it's difficult to monitor test takers. If multiple scenarios are run simultaneously, it may be harder for a single individual to score all the tests, but anonymous identification on the test sheets would also permit students to evaluate and score each other's work as part of the exercise. This too is similar to the NCIDQ in that it is scored by other interior designers and not by NCIDQ staff. Evaluation checklists are included to help students evaluate the projects when they score them.

The multiple-choice questions are distributed in proportions similar to those on recent professional exams. The questions are configured to represent some of the different kinds of complexities that professionals encounter on the NCIDQ, such as having to select the BEST answer from four correct choices and questions worded in the reverse, such as selecting the LEAST likely outcome. Students sometimes find such questions tricky and resent knowing the right answer but getting the question wrong because of the question's structure. This is a safe place for them to practice slowing down and watching out for the question's content. The questions in this exercise do not rely on the judgment that comes with working in the field but rather the information that the student has likely learned in the classroom. If the individual curriculum did not cover the answer of a specific question, the multiple-choice portion may also present a chance to learn some new fact about business, communication skills, or other topics.

The questions on the full version of the multiple-choice test also appear on the lite version. The lite-version questions are easier to answer; the instructor can use these if he or she would rather run a timed exercise to give students a sense of the test's pace. The full version is longer and appropriate if the instructor wants to give students a sense of the test's scale. An answer key with detailed explanations follows each multiple-choice exam.

Many design professionals who have taken the NCIDQ feel that experience and education alone are insufficient for success on the exam. Without specific preparatory exercises, the test is difficult to pass. That is another reason that there are two levels of complexity available for each of the four design scenarios here. The full version of the scenario is similar to the scope and scale of recent tests, and the lite version allows for a timed exercise imitating the time constraints of the NCIDQ exam. Therefore, students can get a sense of the size and scope over a longer exercise duration with a full version and a sense of timing using the lite version of an exercise. It may be helpful for students to work through a long version, allowing two sessions for each part of the exercise, and then completing a different scenario using the lite version, run as a strictly timed exercise to give them a sense of both scale and timing. Both versions are simplified and relative to the actual exam. The accompanying CD-ROM features the Timed Design Exercises at a larger scale. This allows users to view and print the exercises on 11 × 17 paper and practice as needed.

Objectives

The objectives of this book are to:

- Give students a valid senior-level learning experience and decrease trepidation around the professional test.

- Take the mystery out of the NCIDQ exam by providing a mini exam-like experience for interior design students.

- Help students assimilate, analyze, and communicate information in a short period of time.

- Enable students to read the program quickly and develop a design concept that meets all of the design requirements, allowing time to develop and complete the mandatory drawing.

- Help students budget the average time per question, dividing the time allotted by the number of questions.

- Provide a framework for studying and taking the test, including time management.

- Enable students to balance creativity with evidence of ability to respond to a program and integrate design principles, accessible design, and health, safety and welfare issues into a three-dimensional solution.

MULTIPLE-CHOICE EXAM

Full Version

MULTIPLE-CHOICE EXAM

Full Version

Principles and Practices of Interior Design, Full Version

All of the following multiple-choice questions appear on the full version of this student study guide exam. (A Lite Version follows this version.) The multiple-choice answers are listed at the end of this section, and provide an explanation for the instructor as to why the answer is correct.

Elements and Principles of Design

1. To increase the apparent size of a small library you would
   a. paint the shelving units the same light color as the walls.
   b. paint the shelving units and trim in a light color and the walls in a dark color.
   c. paint the shelving units and trim in a dark color and the walls in a light color.
   d. paint the shelving units and the walls the same dark color.

2. At one end of a large dining room in a country club there is a bay window containing a six-top table. To increase the intimacy of a group seated here, you would manipulate the
   a. color.
   b. pattern.
   c. scale.
   d. texture.

3. A stucco wall is one way to create
   a. pattern.
   b. texture.
   c. line.
   d. color.

4. In order to maximize safety and visibility on stairs,
   a. install a carpet with a large pattern as a runner secured with carpet rods.
   b. use a different material on each tread.
   c. highlight the treads and cast the risers in shadow.
   d. install a halogen wall sconce above each tread location.

5. The greatest contrast will be created from
   a. two shades of varying temperature.
   b. two saturated complementary colors.
   c. two tints of varying temperature.
   d. an analogous pair of colors.

6. The *most* effective way to highlight the texture of a fiber artwork would be to
   a. mount a color-corrected fluorescent fixture below and slightly forward of the piece.
   b. mount several low-wattage flood lamps above and 3 feet forward of the piece.
   c. mount an incandescent xenon or halogen strip light above and slightly forward of the piece to graze it with light.
   d. install a cove with indirect light carefully aimed to strike the upper portion of the artwork.

7. To decrease the visual weight and overbearing appearance of a large sofa in a modest condo living room,
   a. paint the walls a pale, cool color and upholster the sofa in a textured chocolate brown.
   b. paper the walls in a small pattern and upholster the sofa in a contrasting color.
   c. paint the walls in the same color family as the sofa fabric with high-value contrast.
   d. match the wall color to the sofa color with a low-sheen formula on walls and matte texture on the sofa.

8. The simplest way to minimize the effect of poorly positioned doors in a room is to

    a. group them into paneling detail units.
    b. paper the walls in a pattern and use coordinating fabric for stationary drapes left and right of doors.
    c. match casings and doors to wall color.
    d. install a picture mold and dado rail.

9. To create visual unity between a spindled staircase and the surrounding space,

    a. use a wallpaper with vertical stripes.
    b. use a foliate-patterned wall covering in a contrasting color.
    c. employ horizontal stripes across from the stairs.
    d. paint the risers to match the treads.

10. When a space requires that furniture be distributed between two halves of a room in an unbalanced way, adjust the visual balance by

    a. simplifying the backgrounds as much as possible.
    b. holding the furniture on the overfurnished half close to the central axis of the room and spread the furniture on the underfurnished side to the perimeter of the space.
    c. installing an ornate chandelier between the two halves.
    d. lower the light level on the underfurnished side.

11. To emphasize the location of the check-in desk at an elegant, traditional hotel

    a. inset arrows of an expensive elegant flooring material to direct patrons to the desk.
    b. use a startling, asymmetrical balance to attract attention to the desk.
    c. position sound system speakers over desk and employ music to call attention to desk location.
    d. use increased light levels at desk and symmetrical balance left and right with the desk in the center.

12. Harmony in a spa setting would be *most* reliant on

    a. consistent proportion throughout.
    b. unity and a variety of well-balances.
    c. consistent scale throughout.
    d. color schemes.

13. To discourage bank patrons from disturbing clerical workers and to cue them toward service managers in an open plan, the best solution would be to

    a. provide visitor chairs upholstered in a color strongly contrasting with surroundings on the traffic side of the service managers' desks.
    b. orient clerical workers so their backs are to patrons.
    c. place an attractive lamp on the service managers' desks.
    d. block entrance to the clerical area with a velvet rope and an attractive sign reading "No entry beyond this point" and have service managers outside that point.

14. Hanging regularly spaced, similar banners along the pedestrian corridor of a strip mall would be most effective in creating

    a. proportion.
    b. variety.
    c. rhythm.
    d. balance.

15. The principles of Japanese floral arrangement rely most on

    a. symmetry and grounding.
    b. asymmetry and movement.
    c. contortion of natural elements.
    d. analogous color and contrasting texture.

16. To increase interaction with a new exhibit in a museum,

    a. place it on a contrasting flooring material.
    b. hang a banner above the ticket desk announcing it.
    c. position it along a main circulation path and highlight it.
    d. place it among unrelated displays.

17. To create a dynamic presentation of space, a designer would employ

    a. diagonal lines.
    b. radial balance.
    c. repetition creating rhythm.
    d. multiple focal points.

18. To enhance the impression of height within a space,

    a. gradually shift the color from cool near the floor to warm near the top.
    b. employ vertical elements that diminish in width as they extend upward.
    c. install a skylight.
    d. employ horizontal stripes near the floor that stop before reaching eye level, and paint the wall above in a cool color.

Human Factors

19. The most important feature of an ergonomically correct chair for the teller of a 24-hour currency exchange would be

    a. adjustability.
    b. lumbar support.
    c. tilt and swivel.
    d. firm cushioning.

20. The designer is likely to use anthropometric data to determine

    a. the allowable projection of a wall sconce in a public corridor.
    b. the width of an exit corridor.
    c. the height and depth of a transaction surface.
    d. the durability of a surfacing material.

21. To maintain thermal comfort for users of a year-round, interior public pool in a northern climate, the simplest and most effective solution is to

    a. paint surfaces a warm, medium-value hue.
    b. install radiant heat coils in benches and pool deck.
    c. rely on a passive solar system of overhangs to block winter sun.
    d. install two lighting systems—fluorescent for summer and incandescent for winter.

22. The ideal height of a keyboard for a computer is

    a. 30 to $32^3/4$ inches.
    b. $28^1/2$ to $32^3/4$ inches.
    c. 26 to $28^1/2$ inches.
    d. 18 to 24 inches.

23. To provide the most comfortable thermal environment for workers of various ages who are performing a variety of tasks, the most successful solution will be to

    a. group sedentary tasks together in zones separate from active tasks in flexible stations with independent heating controls in each zone.
    b. install warm-hued coverings on tack surfaces in stations of workers who prefer higher temperatures.
    c. give individuals control over the damper position of HVAC systems in their personal areas.
    d. install extra outlets for workers' own small fans and heaters.

24. The minimum clear distance from the edge of a table to an obstruction that allows for a user to push back their chair and rise away from a table is

    a. 18 to 24 inches.
    b. 24 to 30 inches.
    c. 30 to 36 inches.
    d. 36 to 40 inches.

25. When arranging study carrels in a public library, mitigate the problem of proximity by

    a. clearly demarcating territory with an enclosure that screens view.
    b. using neutral materials.
    c. using a light-reflecting material on sides of carrel.
    d. selecting durable, easily maintained surfacing material.

26. Encourage tenants to care for public corridors in multiunit housing structures by

    a. utilizing a different color scheme on each floor.
    b. creating a homey atmosphere.
    c. allowing for personalization within the corridor near each entrance to foster feelings of ownership.
    d. encouraging all tenants to vote on selections.

27. In a business environment where negotiations take place, the negotiating parties will be most comfortable with which of the following seating arrangements?

    a. One on the end and one on the nearest right position of a rectangular table
    b. One on the end and one on the nearest left position of a rectangular table
    c. Anyplace around a round table
    d. One on each side (opposite each other) with 40 inches between them at a square or rectangular table

28. The following is *not* part of the programming process:

    a. Establish goals both stated and unstated
    b. Establish which areas of code impact solution
    c. Establish private zones within the footprint
    d. Establish user requirements

29. The following is the *most* appropriate program statement:

    a. Locate adult relaxation space in master suite
    b. Provide audio separation between children's study space and adult relaxation space
    c. Install single door with weather stripping for sound barrier between children's study and adult relaxation spaces
    d. Children's study space to be located in semipublic zone of house

30. The last step in the programming phase is

    a. postoccupancy evaluation.
    b. user survey.
    c. site inspection.
    d. statement of the problem.

31. Which is *most* true?

    a. The program states the problem; the concept suggests a particular approach to solving the problem.
    b. The program tests the validity of the concept.
    c. The program establishes the aesthetic requirements, and the concept establishes functional requirements.
    d. The concept establishes aesthetic requirements, and the program establishes functional requirements.

32. Which of the following cannot be determined without a site visit?

    a. Location of air supplies and returns and the force of the air handled at that location
    b. Availability of natural light
    c. Sources and volume of user noise generated within space
    d. Number of foot-candles available at 30 inches above finished floor from well-maintained lighting systems

33. If you were conducting a programming interview for a souvenir shop, which of the following is *least* important?

    a. Which items are most often purchased on "impulse"
    b. Location of the restrooms
    c. Typical size and type of items for sale
    d. Security needs

34. Which of the following is *most* true?

    a. Structural columns are assessed on a sliding scale with lower floors absorbing more cost burden.
    b. Rentable area is gross area less area occupied by circulation routes, structural columns, and service chases.
    c. The net area is the space usable for the client's functional needs, and the gross area accounts for structural elements and service chases plus additional space to access and circulate within the net space.
    d. Rentable area is gross area less structural columns, furniture locations, traffic corridors, and service chases.

35. The minimum square-foot requirement for a rectangular work station with 15 LF of work surface and 6 LF of file storage would be

    a. 125 SF.
    b. 100 SF.
    c. 75 SF.
    d. 50 SF.

36. The adjacency matrix has identified several *requested* adjacencies that cannot be satisfied within the building footprint. Your best course of action is to

    a. confirm that the adjacencies identified all required physical connection by reviewing the situation with client.

    b. prioritize based on research and solve for maximizing required connections.

    c. identify in specifications one or more alternative routing systems and info-sharing options to eliminate adjacency needs that can't be met by space planning.

    d. interview users for suggestions.

Space Planning

37. In which of the following instances is anthropometric data *least* important in space planning?

    a. Area allocated for electrical and phone systems' control panel location that is accessed only when there is a problem

    b. Warehouse aisle width in a paperboard company where motorized vehicles transport inventory

    c. Height of shelf above washing machine in a motel laundry room

    d. A spacious executive office

38. After the approved block plan of a hotel renovation has established the area to be allocated to the restaurant and kitchen, which of the following has the *most* influence over the planning of the area?

    a. Existing structural columns and structural walls, windows and exit locations

    b. Whether or not the building has landmark status

    c. Locations of existing plumbing

    d. Existing ornate millwork and chandeliers

39. Of the following open office layouts below, which is *most* convenient for a project manager who has numerous staff consultations throughout the day?

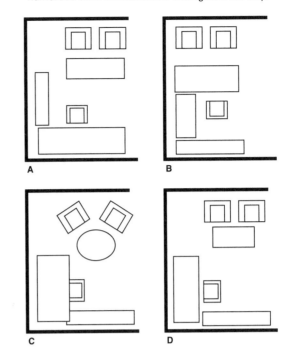

40. A spa in New Mexico with an internal courtyard would suggest what organizational concept for initial planning?

    a. Axial

    b. Central

    c. Radial

    d. Grid

41. The most efficient type of circulation system for high-density closed office layouts is

    a. radial.

    b. grid.

    c. single-loaded corridor.

    d. double-loaded corridor.

42. Before undertaking the space planning for an adaptive reuse situation, an interior designer would have to consult an expert for which of the following?

    a. Number of air supplies and diffusers in the space

    b. Adequate water pressure in washrooms

    c. Feasibility of opening a double-wide door in a load-bearing wall

    d. Presence of adequate electrical outlets to meet local code

43. Which of the following zone considerations is the *least* important for the space planning of an eye surgeon's offices?

    a. Exam vs. surgery
    b. Noisy vs. quiet
    c. Staff vs. patient
    d. Hygienic vs. standard

44. Dead-end corridors in an office building should not exceed how many feet in length?

    a. 20 feet
    b. 30 feet
    c. 40 feet
    d. 50 feet

45. Plans for the expansion of a restaurant require an additional exit. Your primary concern for its location is to

    a. minimize its appearance so patrons do not confuse it with the front door.
    b. ensure that it does not open into an alleyway or onto private property.
    c. keep the location as remote as possible from the existing entrance.
    d. position it as close to the entrance as possible so that patrons are familiar with it and they can find it easily.

Cost Estimating

46. A credenza that lists for $6,000 and is a 40 percent-off item that a designer sells at net plus 30 percent would cost the client before freight, taxes, and delivery

    a. $3,120.
    b. $2,520.
    c. $4,680.
    d. $7,384.

47. If the standard rule of thumb in your area is that a drywall partition costs about $50 per lineal foot regardless of height, and contractors typically charge a 15 percent markup, what will you estimate your client's 12-foot long $\times$ 8-foot tall partition wall will cost?

    a. $90
    b. $720
    c. $690
    d. $1,350

48. Why would a client be likely to act on the designer's suggestion that they purchase appliances directly from the vendor rather than through the contractor?

    a. The designer does not want to be responsible for the performance of the appliances.
    b. The client will save themselves the contractor's markup.
    c. Delivery can be controlled so the appliances are not delivered to a dirty construction site.
    d. There are fewer people involved in the purchase, so there is less opportunity for miscommunication.

49. The most accurate budget figures for a furnishing job can be drawn up by the

    a. furniture manufacturer and interior designer.
    b. general contractor and interior designer.
    c. furniture manufacturer and client.
    d. interior designer and furniture dealer.

50. If you were estimating for a construction project in an unfamiliar city, which of the following would provide the most accurate cost data?

    a. Current cost data book adjusted for location
    b. Interior designer who practices in that area
    c. General contractor who works in that area
    d. Computerized cost-estimating software adjusted for that location

51. Estimate the yardage required to drape a window meeting the following specifications: window is 4 feet wide; when open, the drape is to stack on the wall, not in front of the window. Side hems, overlaps, and returns add 24 inches to the width. Finished length is 7 feet; required hems and headers will add 18 inches. Fabric is 48 inches wide with no repeat and will require two-and-a-half times fullness for the look that you require. The estimate closest to the required yardage to be

    a. 12 yards.
    b. 10 yards.
    c. 8 yards.
    d. 6 yards.

52. Which method of estimating would provide the *most* accurate quantity projection?

    a. Square footage
    b. Quantity takeoff
    c. Rule of thumb
    d. Estimating chart

53. Bids have been submitted by four contractors, and the lowest bid is over budget by 10 percent. The best way to handle the situation is to

    a. contact the lowest bidder and negotiate for the 10 percent cost savings by being prepared to make compromises in quality.
    b. contact the lowest bidder and tell them the job is theirs if they can alter the specs to lower their price by 10 percent.
    c. contact the client and notify them that the project will cost 10 percent more than anticipated and proceed with the project because 10 percent is immaterial.
    d. redesign and adjust specifications to meet the budget.

54. You have specified a 54-inch-wide wall covering for all four walls of a hallway that is 6 feet wide and 50 feet long. The ceiling is 10 feet high. There are eight 36-inch doors. The wall covering is $12 per yard. What is closest to your estimate of the wall covering's cost?

    a. $760
    b. $1,000
    c. $1,344
    d. $4,000

Construction Drawings

55. The location of slab-to-slab partitions dividing a space are most clearly shown on which of the following?

    a. Interior elevations
    b. Interior wall sections
    c. Reflected ceiling plans
    d. Finish plans

56. The above symbol indicates

    a. a building section.
    b. the location of an interior section in the document set.
    c. a detail drawing indicator.
    d. the existence of an elevation view.

57. Who is responsible for verifying that HVAC systems and lighting and equipment do not interfere with each other?

    a. Interior designer
    b. Mechanical/HVAC engineer
    c. Electrical engineer
    d. General contractor

58. The following should be called out in drawings to ensure a good fit between a custom cabinet and the adjoining surface:

    a. Type of fasteners or adhesives to be used (which hold the cabinet together)
    b. Scribe pieces (which span the distance between the cabinet and the wall or ceiling, compensating for the fact that buildings are seldom plumb and square)
    c. Leveling devices (which allow a squared cabinet to relate to a nonsquared ceiling/floor)
    d. Setback reveals (which create a shadow line at the junction between the cabinet and adjoining surfaces)

59. Which of the following allows for the most control from panel to panel in wood paneling fabrication?

    a. Book match
    b. Sequence match
    c. Center butt match
    d. Blueprint match

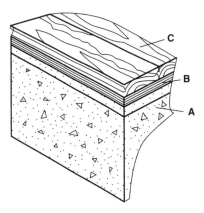

The next four questions relate to the above diagram.

60. The above diagram shows

    a. typical wood floor installation for a detached single-family home.
    b. typical wood floor installation for a multifamily residential building.
    c. wood floor system with a sound barrier over concrete.
    d. glue-down wood floor installation for retrofit situation.

61. In the above diagram, "A" represents

    a. sound-deadening material.
    b. concrete slab.
    c. original terrazzo floor with new surface adhered.
    d. thickset.

62. In the above diagram, "B" represents

    a. plywood subfloor.
    b. particle board interlayer.
    c. MDF substrate.
    d. undetermined engineered substrate.

63. In the above diagram, "C" illustrates

    a. engineered flooring product.
    b. rift-sawn wood.
    c. plain-sawn oak.
    d. dimensional wood strip flooring.

Construction Specifications

64. Which item in the following specification excerpt is a performance specification?

Part 2 Products
   2.01 Metal Support material
   General: to the extent not otherwise indicated, comply with ASTM C754 for metal system supporting gypsum wallboard
   Ceiling suspension main runners: 1-1/2-inch steel channels, cold rolled
   Hanger wire: ASTM A641, soft, Class 1 galvanized pre-stretched, sized in accordance with ASTM C754
   Hanger anchorage devices: size for 3 times calculated loads, except size direct-pull concrete inserts for 5 times calculated loads
   Studs: ASTM C645; 25 gauge, 2-1/2 inches deep, except as otherwise indicated
   Runners: Match studs; type recommended by stud manufacturer for vertical abutment of drywall work at other work

    a. Ceiling suspension main runners
    b. Hanger wire
    c. Hanger anchorage devices
    d. Hanger wire

65. What is the best way to ensure that the new millwork on a remodeling project matches existing, which was installed 20 years ago?

    a. State on the drawings and specifications that new work is to match existing
    b. Ask the painter or party responsible for finishes to investigate original formulas, deduce the formulation, and duplicate that formula on new work
    c. Ask the client for records of original formula and forward them to the painter
    d. Forward a material sample to manufacturers of similar products and request that they forward specifications from their specification master for appropriate product

66. Specifications can be written very concisely the following way:

    a. Omit conjunctions
    b. Rewrite descriptions for performance, omitting manufacturer's adjectives
    c. Use industry buzzwords that sum up rather than fully explain
    d. Refer to standards delineated in other documents without spelling them out in your document

67. What does the term "approved equal" mean when it appears in a specification?

    a. The client and designer must both agree upon the specification
    b. The contractor may substitute any product with similar specifications
    c. A specification has been given, but the contractor may submit alternatives for approval
    d. The client and the designer have reserved the right to change the specification after the work has begun

68. What is the best way to ensure that the exact product you want will be installed?

    a. Write a descriptive specification including performance requirements
    b. Write a proprietary specification including all manufacturers' ID numbers
    c. Require that material be returnable at designer's discretion
    d. Include a picture of the item in schedules prepared for bid

69. You have been informed that the material you specified for countertops has been back ordered and may arrive too late to complete the project by the deadline. The best course of action is to

    a. wait for it to ship before raising false alarms.
    b. secure temporary material.
    c. revise the construction schedule.
    d. contact the client immediately with possible solutions and determine a course of action.

70. Which of the following would not be found in the project manual?

    a. Concept imagery guiding development of the design
    b. Testing data related to materials specified
    c. Installation information for materials
    d. Instructions to bidders

71. You are specifying multiple wall finishes to be used in an irregularly shaped office. The best way to convey the information so the correct finish material is used on each surface is

    a. conducting an on-site walk-through with the painting contractor and using verbal instructions.
    b. designating N, S, E, W, on the finish schedule.
    c. specifying your office as the ship-to location so the material cannot be installed until you have reviewed location with installers.
    d. using a combination of lines, symbols, and elevations to show clearly in the document set where each material is to be used.

72. Per the build-out agreement, your client's landlord will prime and paint walls. Your client would like to have his own paperhanger install a specialty wall covering in the conference room. What is the best way to ensure the walls are properly prepared for a secure wall covering installation?

    a. Information regarding special sizing required should be forwarded to landlord's painters and added to their work.
    b. Client should not pull the work out of contract but should allow the landlord's painter to install and be responsible for the work.
    c. Walls should be primed by the landlord's painting contractor but sized by the paperhanger.
    d. Priming formulation should be forwarded to paper manufacturer for written approval prior to substituting the primer for sizing.

SECTION II
Contract Development and Administration

Contract Documents

73. Which of the following are legally binding?

    a. Specifications
    b. Schedules
    c. Drawings
    d. All of the above

74. Which of the following is not part of the contract documents?

    a. Any addenda modifying the original contact
    b. The contractor's estimate
    c. Specifications
    d. Contract between the owner and the contractor

75. During the contract administration (implementation) of a project, the designer is responsible for

    a. furniture specifications.
    b. coordination of trades.
    c. meeting with the general contractor and conducting site visits.
    d. finish specifications.

76. Who is responsible for safety at the job site?

    a. Architect
    b. General contractor
    c. Interior designer
    d. Owner

77. The finish plan will be used by the

    a. carpenter.
    b. electrician.
    c. furniture installer.
    d. painter/paperhanger.

78. In a typical set of construction drawings, sheets will be ordered as follows:

    a. Title and index page, then floor plans, then reflected ceiling plans
    b. Floor plans, then details, then elevations all indexed at the end
    c. Title and index page, then sections, then elevations
    d. Floor plans, then electrical plan, then elevations

79. A specification that requires a carpet that is ASTM E648 is

    a. proprietary.
    b. descriptive.
    c. a performance standard.
    d. a reference standard.

80. NIC means

    a. no interior contract.
    b. not in contract.
    c. not in compliance.
    d. not intended for construction.

81. After a contract for build-out has been awarded and shop drawings have been approved, you notice some errors on the cabinet shop drawings that you had previously missed. The correct course of action at this point would be to issue

    a. a stop-work order, because the work is not in compliance with your original intentions.
    b. a notice of error to the cabinet shop, because their shop drawings are in error.
    c. a change order, because you already approved proceeding with these plans so are now changing the contracted procedure.
    d. an addendum, because your intentions modify their understanding of the scope of work.

Furniture Fixtures and Equipment

82. Which of the following would you specify for upholstery in a family-style restaurant?

    a. Silk/wool blend
    b. Wool/nylon blend
    c. Cotton/rayon blend
    d. Acrylic/acetate blend

83. What performance tests should you specify for fabric used in the multipurpose room of a community center?

    a. Double-rubs and NRC
    b. Indentation load deflection and SRC
    c. PSI and Fade-O-Meter
    d. Wyzenbeeck and fading

84. How would you prioritize characteristics for the learning carrels in a high school library?

    a. Durability, then cost, then design particulars
    b. Flammability, then design details, then comfort
    c. Finish, then cost, then design
    d. Washability, then comfort, then finish

85. Which of the following should you be *least* likely to specify for a sunroom sofa?

    a. Rayon
    b. Polyester
    c. Modacrylic
    d. Acrylic

86. Which type of cushioning would be *most* suitable for the furniture in the waiting room of an ophthalmologist's office?

    a. Down-wrapped foam
    b. Cotton batting
    c. Low-density urethane
    d. High-density foam

87. In which environment would you expect the most stringent safety standards?

    a. Residential single-family detached buildings
    b. Mercantile spaces
    c. Hospitals
    d. Commercial spaces

88. Class A fabric will not

    a. rot.
    b. ignite.
    c. char.
    d. smolder.

89. Which of the following has the greatest impact on the flammability of upholstered furniture?

    a. Fabric fiber content
    b. Fabric and interliner
    c. Frame design and material and fabric
    d. Cushioning (padding) type and fabric flammability rating

90. You are designing dressers to be mass-produced for dormitories at a state university. You would specify

    a. dovetailed, hardwood drawer boxes, 45-pound particle board substrate with high-pressure laminate.
    b. dovetailed hardwood drawer boxes, 35-pound particle board substrate with low-pressure laminate.
    c. marine-grade plywood drawers and cases with low-pressure laminate over all surfaces.
    d. solid wood drawers and cases with five coats of clear spar varnish.

Interior Construction

91. Which type of locking device is most appropriate for an office building?

   a. Cylindrical lock
   b. Tubular lock
   c. Card reader
   d. Mortise lock

The next two questions relate to the following diagram.

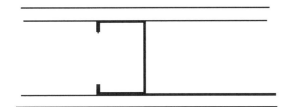

92. What type of partition is indicated by the above diagram?

   a. $3\frac{1}{2}$-inch wooden stud with $\frac{5}{8}$-inch gypsum wallboard
   b. $1\frac{1}{2}$-inch metal stud with two layers of $\frac{1}{2}$-inch gypsum wallboard
   c. $3\frac{5}{8}$-inch metal stud with $\frac{5}{8}$-inch gypsum wallboard
   d. $3\frac{1}{2}$-inch wooden stud with wood paneling

93. It has a fire rating of

   a. 1 hour.
   b. 2 hour.
   c. 4 hour.
   d. It is not suitable for a rated partition.

94. Which method of veneer slicing would you specify for the straightest grain?

   a. Plain sawn
   b. Rift sawn
   c. Flat slicing
   d. Rotary slicing

95. To detail a door frame for a conference room where audio privacy is critical, which of the following is *least* likely to be required?

   a. Neoprene gasketing
   b. Solid-core door
   c. Heavy-duty silent door closer
   d. Astragals between pairs

96. If a client wanted to remove a partition that may be a load-bearing wall, what is your best course of action?

   a. Send a letter to the building department in that jurisdiction so they can adjust their records relative to that building
   b. Review original building plans to confirm the wall's purpose
   c. Have an engineer or architect review the problem and make a recommendation
   d. Look in the attic to determine what loads are being borne by the partition

97. Safety glazing is likely not required in which of the following locations?

   a. Glass serving as railing on a staircase
   b. Shower doors
   c. Full-height glass sidelights next to a solid wood door
   d. Sidelights in a residential door unit where the sill is greater than 18 inches AFF

Finishes

98. In order to allow your client to easily change the wallpaper above the chair rail in her dining room, you would specify

   a. pre-pasted.
   b. peelable.
   c. Type II vinyl.
   d. laminated paper.

99. For greatest durability in the service corridor for an office with wheeled cart traffic, you would specify

   a. Type III vinyl wall covering.
   b. Type A vinyl wall cover.
   c. Type I commercial grade wall covering.
   d. pre-pasted paper.

100. The most functional floor for the entrance to a nature preserve's education center would be

   a. unfilled travertine.
   b. polished granite.
   c. granite with a flamed finish.
   d. mesh-mounted river rock in mortar.

101. When your residential clients request wood flooring, they most often have in mind

    a. wood parquet flooring.
    b. laminated flooring with a wood veneer face.
    c. wood plank flooring.
    d. 2¼-inch wood strip flooring.

102. Your design firm is coordinating surfacing selections with the architect's details. You have in mind to use an ungauged, cleft-face slate floor over concrete slab in a client's sunroom. Which installation method will be most successful?

    a. ½-inch thick mortar bed to prevent cracks with dry-set stone on top
    b. Thickset with a cleavage membrane under the stone to prevent cracks
    c. Thin-set installation with unsanded grout
    d. Floating floor installation with ½-inch cork underlayment

103. In a commercial kitchen, you would specify the following flooring:

    a. Cork tile with an oil finish
    b. ⅛-inch thick self-adhesive vinyl tile
    c. Sheet vinyl
    d. Sheet rubber

104. Which of the following will provide the *least* successful installation of carpet for hotel corridors over concrete subfloors?

    a. Wool carpet installed glue-down
    b. Acrylic carpet installed glue-down
    c. Nylon carpet stretched in over felt cushion
    d. Nylon carpet installed glue-down

105. To ensure that windowpaning of grout (grout clings to tile face and remains after cleaning) around tile perimeters is not a problem on a tile installation,

    a. dry-fit all tiles prior to adhering.
    b. specify unsanded grout.
    c. match grout to color of tile.
    d. specify grout release.

106. You are carefully matching wood finishes throughout a space. In order to ensure that the appearance remains as consistent as possible over time, you will do the following:

    a. Specify a variety of gloss levels and tint the sealant or stain the wood
    b. Consistently use solids or veneers of the same species with the same formulation with UV protection for sealant
    c. Use a lacquer finish on some items so there is less wood, and seal with a sealant with UV protection
    d. Use a closed pore finish with filler matched from one surface to the next

Lighting

107. What is the most important criterion when specifying lighting for a fabric showroom?

    a. Color temperature
    b. Visual comfort
    c. Color rendering index
    d. Coefficient of utilization

108. The best light source for highlighting the crystal in a department store would be

    a. 75-watt MR-16 for sparkle.
    b. incandescent A-19 for ease of maintenance.
    c. cool-white deluxe fluorescent for economy.
    d. metal halide for brightness.

109. The graphics studio you are designing will require a work area where print media campaigns are laid out. What lighting problem would you anticipate for this work area?

    a. Excessive brightness ratio
    b. Inadequate brightness ratio
    c. Direct glare
    d. Indirect glare/veiling reflection

110. It is quite common for office tasks to combine review of printed material with work at the computer. Which of the following would be the most appropriate approach to lighting the space?

    a. Direct/indirect controlled at each station
    b. Low-brightness troffers on dimmer switches and a task light at each station
    c. Indirect ambient light with an adjustable task light at each station
    d. Adjustable downlights over desks and indirect light on each terminal

111. The operating costs of the lighting scheme that you have devised for a retail environment have come in over the allowed budget for operating costs. Which of the following is the best first approach to reducing operating cost?

    a. Space fixtures farther apart
    b. Search for lamps with higher efficiency and longer life
    c. Replace all incandescent fixtures with fluorescents
    d. Alter the task/ambient system

112. Who would be responsible for the installation details of computerized control equipment, circuitry, and light-fixture installation details for a large commercial installation?

    a. Electrical contractor
    b. Interior designer
    c. General contractor
    d. Electrical engineer

113. You are an in-house designer for a hospital and are overseeing the programming of an automated system to control light levels in a long narrow waiting area. There is a window at the far end, near lounge seating and a table and chairs near the corridor end. You would probably program for a system that will

    a. use lower light levels during the day and higher light levels after dark.
    b. raise light levels at the table near the corridor and lower them at the lounge seating near the window when it's bright outside.
    c. utilize slow fade to vary the light levels, alternating back and forth between the lounge and table area.
    d. always maintain higher light levels at the lounge seating than the table, as the systems vary the light levels throughout the day and night.

114. To take advantage of the visual characteristics of an existing brick wall in a 7-foot-wide by 50-foot-long hallway for an adaptive reuse project you would

    a. graze the surface with direct downlight from a concealed source.
    b. graze the surface with direct uplight.
    c. use indirect light.
    d. wash the surface with light from above and below.

115. When lighting stairs, it is most important to provide

    a. 100-foot lamberts on treads.
    b. 100 foot-candles on treads.
    c. contrast between risers and treads.
    d. indirect lighting on risers.

Mechanical and Electrical Systems

116. Fire code prohibits which of the following in a return-air plenum?

    a. Unsheathed low-voltage wire
    b. Electrical conduit
    c. Water pipes
    d. Wood blocking

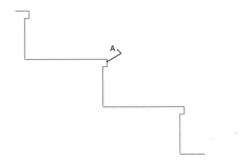

117. In the above diagram, "A" is indicating the

    a. stringer.
    b. riser.
    c. nosing.
    d. toe clip.

118. When specifying a new window covering to replace the building standard, which of the following approvals is *least* important?

    a. Architect's approval that the new treatments will not adversely affect heating the glass
    b. Mechanical engineer's approval related to heating and cooling loads
    c. Building owner's approval related to exterior appearance
    d. Lighting designer's approval of the new reflectance impact on lighting

119. The above symbol indicates

    a. recessed floor data line.
    b. ceiling-suspended exit light.
    c. wall washer or adjustable light fixture.
    d. emergency lighting.

120. Your plans to join two stacked condominium units together require that a stair opening be created between the two units. The slab-to-slab dimension is 9 feet, 8 inches, and the slab is 10 inches thick. What is the best riser/tread combination?

    a. 7-inch riser and 8-inch tread
    b. 8-inch riser and 10-inch tread
    c. 8-inch riser and 12-inch tread
    d. 7-inch riser and 11-inch tread

121. When laying out the stacks in a public library, with whom would you consult regarding location of shelving?

    a. Structural engineer
    b. Fire marshal
    c. Library of Congress numerical system coordinator
    d. HVAC engineer

122. If all the following answer choices were present in the CFO's new corner office, which one is *most* likely to require modification in order to provide acoustical privacy?

    a. Gypsum board and metal stud partition between this office and the next
    b. Convector running continuously under all the windows on that level
    c. Clear glass door between the office and the corridor
    d. Acoustical ceiling suspended to 8 feet AFF concealing a 3-foot plenum

123. Which of the following would be prohibited under the panels of an access floor in an office for a stock-trading company?

    a. Plumbing pipe
    b. Electrical conduit
    c. Computer cable
    d. Low-voltage wire

124. In a plenum ceiling space, which handles air for the HVAC system, how would you prevent a fire from spreading horizontally?

    a. Pack the plenum with fiberglass insulation
    b. Bolt a fire damper to the underside of the floor slab above
    c. Use a fire-rated panel system and run it up to the upper slab
    d. Install sprinklers above and below the finished ceiling

Acoustics

125. A "floating floor" system with a sound abatement may contribute to sound control in high-rise buildings by

    a. minimizing impact against the floor surface.
    b. creating a sound baffle with insulation.
    c. preventing sound leaks where plumbing pipe penetrates the deck.
    d. preventing sound from telegraphing through materials.

126. The ratings most important to reducing sound moving from one space to another through the floor materials would be

    a. NRC (noise reduction coefficient) and IIC (impact isolation class)
    b. STC (sound transmission class) and IIC
    c. NRC and STC
    d. NC (noise criteria) and NRC

127. Changing a ceiling from gypsum board to acoustical tile would most affect the room's

    a. reverberation.
    b. noise criteria curve.
    c. transmission.
    d. impact insulation class.

128. Which of the following is *least* effective in reducing noise moving between two spaces?

    a. Increase transmission loss of the wall separating the two spaces
    b. Use resilient channels to reduce the overall stiffness of the wall
    c. Decrease the surface area of the shared wall
    d. Use sound-absorptive material on both sides of the wall

129. In a small performance space, it would be best to avoid

    a. amplifiers.
    b. parallel walls.
    c. well-positioned oblique angles.
    d. carpeting.

130. Which is the most accurate statement?

    a. A good acoustical material absorbs all frequencies equally.
    b. Reduce sound by at least 10 decibels to produce a noticable difference.
    c. A good acoustical configuration eliminates all background noise.
    d. Use live surfaces to distort sound waves but not eliminate them.

131. The most cost-efficient way of eliminating airborne noise through the wall between two spaces is to

    a. replace tempered glass with laminated glass.
    b. curve the space around the noise source.
    c. use a double-stud wall construction.
    d. avoid back-to-back electrical boxes.

132. White noise is desirable in office situations because

    a. it improves acoustical privacy.
    b. it improves concentration and reduces monotony.
    c. its presence causes users to perceive the space as "elegant."
    d. it masks the hum of electrical equipment.

133. What is the purpose of insulating interior walls?

    a. To improve the acoustical characteristics of the space
    b. To absorb sound energy being transmitted through the wall
    c. To reflect sound back into noisy spaces
    d. To reduce impact transmission

Communication Methods

134. A drawing that produces a 3-D view that can be measured with a scale ruler at any location in the drawing is considered

    a. an orthographic projection.
    b. a two-point perspective.
    c. an oblique drawing.
    d. isometric.

135. A drawing that produces a 3-D view that creates a strong emphasis/focal-point location in the picture plane is a(n)

    a. two-point perspective.
    b. one-point perspective.
    c. oblique drawing.
    d. orthographic projection.

136. Perspective drawings are the most easily understood by clients because

    a. they are most like the way we perceive space and objects.
    b. they are the fastest way to show the organization of the space.
    c. they are the most accurate in portraying scale.
    d. multiple viewpoints are available within a single drawing.

137. A bird's-eye view is most accurately shown by

    a. a two-point perspective.
    b. an orthographic projection.
    c. an isometric.
    d. a plan view.

138. In a line drawing, a hierarchy of information can be conveyed by

    a. varying the level of detail so objects in front are more detailed.
    b. varying the value so objects in back are darker.
    c. using a variety of line weights to emphasize important elements.
    d. adding symbols to drawings as an aid to organization.

139. In a two-point perspective with vanishing points outside of the drawing sheet (wide-spaced), an adjustment is typically required to correct distortion in what area of the picture plane?

    a. Toward the bottom and top of the drawing sheet
    b. At the left and right of the drawing sheet
    c. At the apex
    d. At the junction where two vertical planes meet

140. The two views that are most similar in the information they present are

    a. one-point perspective and orthogonal.
    b. elevation and vertical section.
    c. isometric and one-point perspective.
    d. floor plan and site plan.

141. The accuracy of which drawing is confirmed with a grid?

    a. Isometric
    b. Floor plan
    c. Perspective
    d. Orthogonal projection

142. Which of the following is *least* true of drawings?

    a. Proportions of items in a space are best compared in a plan view.
    b. A good drawing answers all questions generated by its existence.
    c. Inserting a human form can help describe scale of a space presented.
    d. One 3-D view is better than two 2-D views to describe the junction between two planes.

143. Which of the following is the best reason to create a perspective drawing?

    a. To show how a piece of manufactured furniture looks
    b. To show the texture of a material
    c. To compare the relative construction details of two items
    d. To present an item or space that does not exist in the physical world

Building Codes

144. When referring to the code book for codes pertaining to a loft conversion for a seven-story brick building with wooden posts and flooring systems to be occupied by business tenants providing services, you would refer to

    a. masonry construction, mercantile, and high-rise classifications.
    b. heavy timber and masonry, business, and high-rise classifications.
    c. masonry construction business and low-rise classifications.
    d. fire-resistive, service occupancy, and high-rise classifications.

145. Where are flame-spread ratings most restrictive in all building and occupancy classification types?

    a. In enclosed areas
    b. In unfamiliar locations
    c. In exit enclosures
    d. On corridor floors

146. Which test gives the most accurate evaluation of the safety of a partition wall?

    a. ASTM E-84, which tests the surface burning characteristics of building materials
    b. Steiner Tunnel Test, which tests flame spread on a surfacing material
    c. Methenamine pill test, which tests flame spread on a surfacing material
    d. ASTM E-119, which tests the fire resistance of building constructions and materials

147. The minimum number of toilet fixtures required for a retrofit project is best determined by

    a. occupancy load and occupancy group.
    b. accessibility requirements and building type.
    c. building type and square footage.
    d. occupancy load and grandfather clause.

148. When selecting new finishes for a completed space to bring it into compliance with flame-spread standards, the most important considerations are

    a. hourly rating of the partition on which the finish will be placed.
    b. whether or not the building use classification will change in the future or if a sprinkler system may one day be installed.
    c. occupancy group determining required fire resistance and where each finish will be located in the project.
    d. if the space has a plenum ceiling.

149. The ASTM (American Society for Testing and Materials) is a(n)

    a. industry standards-writing organization.
    b. model code group.
    c. federal code writing agency.
    d. nonprofit group dedicated to building safety.

150. If you were specifying safety glass for a location where breaking and entering was *not* the primary concern, what types of glass would you consider?

    a. Tempered and wire
    b. Tempered and ballistic
    c. Laminated and wire
    d. Tempered and laminated

151. Dead-end corridors in sprinklered buildings may be a maximum of

    a. 5 feet.
    b. 20 feet.
    c. 60 feet.
    d. 100 feet.

152. Exits in a restaurant may never pass through

    a. lobbies.
    b. service corridors.
    c. bar areas.
    d. kitchens.

153. Which is the *most* correct statement about exit corridors?

    a. They are calculated as required width plus door swings.
    b. They must be used for only egress.
    c. They must be enclosed by fire-rated partitions.
    d. They need not be accessible.

154. Exit doors must be _____-inches wide doors with a free clear width of _____ inches and measure no greater than _____ inches per single leaf.

    a. 34/30/50
    b. 36/32/48
    c. 32/30/50
    d. 30/28/48

155. Use the following table to calculate the occupant load of a supper club on the ground floor with 4,000 square feet of dining area, 1,000 square feet of kitchen, a 1,000-square-foot bar, and a 1,000-square-foot dance floor.

    a. 465
    b. 380
    c. 479
    d. 395

Use	Occupancy Load Factor

Assembly areas, concentrated use (without fixed seats)
    Auditoriums
    Dance floors
    Lodge rooms
	7

Assembly areas, less-concentrated use
    Conference rooms
    Dining rooms
    Drinking establishments
    Exhibit rooms
    Lounges
    Stages
	15

Hotels and apartments	200
Kitchens—commercial	200
Offices	100
Stores, ground floor	30

156. The rise of a stairway means the

    a. distance measured from nosing to nosing.
    b. total of one riser plus two treads.
    c. total of two risers plus one tread.
    d. distance from finished slab to finished slab.

157. You are developing the space planning for a full-floor tenant in a high-rise building. What two things must you know to determine travel distance?

    a. The building type and what the occupancy classification is
    b. Building orientation and whether the building is sprinklered
    c. Height of the building and construction type
    d. Height of the building and whether the building is sprinklered

158. Which of the following is most important for determining the number of exits that are required from a space?

    a. ADA classification
    b. Occupant load
    c. Distance from room exit to building exit
    d. Exit widths

159. Corridor widths are primarily controlled by

    a. occupancy load.
    b. length of exit travel.
    c. building-use classification.
    d. building-type classification.

Barrier Free

160. The minimum clear floor space required for a wheelchair is

    a. 36 by 40 inches.
    b. 36 by 48 inches.
    c. 30 by 40 inches.
    d. 30 by 48 inches.

161. The minimum depth (not height) required under accessible lavatories is

    a. 12 inches.
    b. 17 inches.
    c. 20 inches.
    d. 24 inches.

162. How high will you mount a grab bar in a barrier-free commercial restroom?

    a. 20 inches
    b. 30 inches
    c. 36 inches
    d. 40 inches

163. The best type of sink in a barrier-free design is

    a. wall-hung with shroud.
    b. pedestal.
    c. freestanding.
    d. vanity with shroud.

164. The minimum clear width for a door should be

    a. 30 inches.
    b. 32 inches.
    c. 34 inches.
    d. 36 inches.

165. When designing a hotel that will accommodate the disabled, which of the following would be *most* important to include?

    a. Visual alarms and flashing smoke detectors
    b. Tactile signage and audible alarms
    c. Audible alarms and large, contrasted lettering on signage
    d. Audible and visual alarms

166. When considering the initial space planning of a handicapped-accessible toilet, which of the following is of most concern?

    a. Possible door swings and clearances required for optional approaches
    b. Stall depth and grab-bar height
    c. Door swing and stall depth
    d. Clear space at jamb and turning radius

167. Measured from the nosing to the center of the handrail, which height will meet universal design concepts?

    a. 30 to 38 inches
    b. 34 to 38 inches
    c. 34 to 48 inches
    d. 28 to 45 inches

168. When planning for the updating of a commercial building's entrance to meet code, you realize you can't provide the required clearance next to a door. Which of the following is the best solution?

    a. Switch the current door unit with an existing window unit, which is wider even though the door is now a little too small
    b. Review structural drawings and devise options for widening the current door unit
    c. Swing the door in the opposite direction, even though it is a little less convenient once you get inside
    d. Specify a power-assisted door opener that meets accessibility standards

Owner-Designer Agreements

169. Which of the following is a reimbursable expense?

    a. Copying costs
    b. Producing a study model for space-planning purposes
    c. Extra liability insurance required specifically for the project
    d. A temporary worker to assemble multiple spec books for a meeting

170. The bid has been awarded but construction has not started, and your client has just requested vaguely-defined major changes to the project. The first thing you should do is

    a. notify the contractor that major changes will be made and portions of the work will be rebid.
    b. inform the client that major changes will delay the project and will affect fees.
    c. estimate the additional cost of the changes and receive approval from the client to proceed with redesign.
    d. return all samples and shop drawings for affected areas without approving them.

171. The designer specified manufactured case goods for a niche that was built according to the designer's drawings. The dimensions of the case goods are called out on the furnishings page of the document set that was on the site for construction purposes. The case goods do not fit into the niche. Who pays for correcting the problem?

    a. General contractor
    b. Carpentry subcontractor
    c. Designer
    d. Owner

172. Which type of fee is *least* advantageous to the designer?

    a. Hourly rate
    b. Flat fee
    c. Retail
    d. Hourly with a not-to-exceed cap

173. Which document is used to release funds for the purchase of furniture?

    a. Application for payment
    b. Purchase order
    c. Bill of lading
    d. Final invoice

174. The project construction budget prepared by a design or architectural firm is unlikely to include

    a. designer's fees and reimbursables.
    b. contractor's profit.
    c. cost for obtaining permits.
    d. cost for bringing services to the unit.

175. In order to meet all program requirements, a load-bearing partition must be partially removed. The best course of action is

    a. the client hires an architect to draw up the required plans.
    b. the designer or client hires a structural engineer to draw up the plans.
    c. the contractor devises a way to safely modify the partition.
    d. the owner assumes responsibility for the structure, and the work proceeds as drawn by the designer.

176. Which of the following is *not* true under standard agreements?

    a. The owner is responsible for removal of all equipment and furniture in the facilities to be modified under the contract.
    b. The owner must furnish all legal and insurance counseling required by the project.
    c. The owner's budget must provide for contingencies.
    d. The owner may not abandon the project at any phase after the design contract has been signed.

Professional Practice

177. Which type of insurance is *not* ultimately the client's responsibility to fund?

    a. Property
    b. Workers' compensation
    c. Errors and omissions
    d. General liability

178. Which business organization allows the most control by its founders?

    a. Partnership
    b. Professional corporation
    c. S corporation
    d. C corporation

179. The furniture has been delivered to the job site and signed for by the owner before final inspection and acceptance. Damage is discovered on the some of the furniture finishes. Who is responsible for correcting the damage?

    a. The owner
    b. The furniture dealer
    c. The trucking company
    d. The general contractor

180. Which type of insurance is *least* necessary for a design firm whose employees travel by car to job sites?

    a. General liability
    b. Workers' compensation
    c. Automobile
    d. Employee health insurance

181. Which of the following is *not* considered a trade resource?

    a. Marketing and PR
    b. Custom fabricator
    c. Furniture showroom
    d. Furniture dealer

182. You presented plans and selections to your client, who tells you to "proceed with the work presented." You submit purchase orders and order the items based on your conversation and a deposit check. When the furniture arrives, the client does not like some of the pieces and refuses to pay for them. Your best course of action is:

    a. remind the client that they were approved and you were authorized to purchase them.
    b. forward the sample board from the presentation to the client with a reminder of the approval.
    c. convince the client to accept the furniture, because no specific sales agreement was signed by the client describing the pieces in contention, but you will still have to pay for them.
    d. pay restocking charges on the pieces and furnish alternate selections for approval.

183. You receive a call from a client who would like to engage your services because they are dissatisfied with their current designer. You should

    a. mediate the dispute as a professional courtesy.
    b. tell the owner that you would be happy to discuss the project after the relationship with the current designer has been severed.
    c. suggest that you collaborate with the current designer to complete the project to the client's satisfaction.
    d. enter into a contract with the client that defines which functions will be fulfilled by which designer during the overlap phase.

184. The most appropriate marketing plan for a new design firm would be

    a. an identity package and brochure with services offered.
    b. stationery and business cards.
    c. print media ads in consumer publications.
    d. direct-mail ad campaign.

185. Which of the following is *not* true of a corporation?

    a. Generally taxed at a lower rate than individuals
    b. If sued, stockholder assets are not at risk
    c. Might have only one person in the whole corporation
    d. They are the easiest business form to set up

Project Coordination

186. If a doorway is correctly installed by the contractor and is per the designer's drawings but is later determined by the building inspector to be too narrow, who is responsible for correcting the situation?

    a. The owner
    b. The contractor
    c. The designer
    d. The door fabricator

187. A shop drawing for a custom door is produced by the door manufacturer and was ordered through the general contractor. The interior designer failed to find an error in a dimension stringer. The frame that was produced in accordance with the drawing did not fit the opening that was to receive it. Who is responsible for correcting the mistake?

    a. The general contractor
    b. The interior designer
    c. The framing contractor
    d. The door fabricator

188. Which of the following is not part of the post occupancy evaluation?

    a. Review of the effectiveness of this HVAC system
    b. Interview with representative users of the project
    c. A check on maintenance problems
    d. Suggestions to the client for future projects at the site

189. The furniture contractor can legitimately request which of the following?

    a. Final inspection and acceptance by the owner prior to furniture installation
    b. Extra storage space for furniture that has been delivered to the site
    c. Extra insurance for goods in transit from the warehouse to the site
    d. Additional workers for initial preparation of furniture

190. If some millwork, purchased through the general or furniture contractor, was installed with an incorrect finish and the shop had never forwarded a sample to the interior designer, who is responsible for correcting the problem?

    a. The interior designer
    b. The owner
    c. The contractor
    d. The millworker

191. Which of the following is the *least* important task for the project manager?

    a. Planning weekly use of staff time
    b. Staying current with the client's opinion of how the job is progressing
    c. Keeping notes on all conversations and meeting summaries
    d. Organizing the layout of the construction drawing set

192. During a weekly inspection, you notice a hazardous work condition. You should

    a. point it out to the contractor.
    b. point it out to the contractor and write a letter to the client describing what you saw.
    c. write a letter to the client describing what you saw.
    d. write a letter to the contractor describing what you saw.

193. During the administration phase of the project, the interior designer is primarily responsible for

    a. confirming that work is in accordance with the contract documents.
    b. checking on the quality and quantity of work.
    c. confirming appropriateness of the means, methods, techniques, and procedures of the work.
    d. acts or omissions of contractors or suppliers carrying out the work.

194. Which of the following is most true of furniture delivery and inspection?

    a. The owner always has final say as to which items are acceptably free of damage.
    b. The interior designer always has final say as to which items are acceptably free of damage.
    c. The delivery people are responsible for inspection and touch-up of minor damage in addition to alerting seller in case of major damage.
    d. Manufacturers are liable for damage if items are shipped FOB, Free/Freight on Board their dock.

195. Contract documents are prepared by the interior designer. If a dispute interpreting the contract documents arises between the contractor and owner,

    a. the designer works with the owner to get what is needed from the contractor.
    b. they are referred to the interior designer who must be impartial while rendering a decision about what is most consistent with the intent of the contract documents.
    c. the designer issues a stop-work order until the owner and contractor come to agreement about how the work should be completed.
    d. a middle ground is established and all parties work toward that new goal.

196. The interior designer may *not* withhold approval of a payout to a contractor for which of the following:

    a. Reasonable evidence that the work will not be completed on time
    b. Reasonable evidence that the work cannot be completed for the unpaid balance of the contract sum
    c. The punch list hasn't been completed 100 percent
    d. Probability of third-party claims

ANSWER KEY TO MULTIPLE-CHOICE EXAM

Full Version

Elements and Principles of Design

1. (a) Contrast and dark colors visually shrink spaces.

2. (c) Scale has the most powerful impact on perception of size.

3. (b) Stucco is a plastic material (until it cures), so it is capable of being worked into various textures that can be seen as patterns but are mainly texture.

4. (c) Patterns and color changes may be visually confusing to some users, and a sconce at each tread is excessive. Illuminating treads and contrasting these with shadow on the risers will create the best distinction between risers and treads.

5. (b) Complementary colors will vary in hue and temperature, and often in value as well, so they present the most contrast.

6. (c) Option c will graze the textile with light, which is most effective in highlighting texture.

7. (d) Contrast will emphasize the sofa, so minimize the visual presence of the sofa by minimizing contrast and increasing visual similarity between the sofa and the background.

8. (c) Minimize contrasts to avoid emphasizing door locations by painting the doors and casing in a color that will not contrast with walls (which would accent the door locations).

9. (a) Similarity creates unity, and spindles and vertical stripes have the most in common.

10. (b) Increase the perceived weight in the sparsely furnished side by moving furnishings away from the center, and increase the perception of space on the heavily furnished side by surrounding the grouping with empty area.

11. (d) Arrows in the floor and asymmetrical balance are out of character for an elegant traditional hotel, and speakers would interfere with conversation at the desk. Light is a powerful way to emphasize and will best draw attention to the desk.

12. (b) Harmony is most often described as the perfect balance between unity and variety, so of the options listed, unity has the most impact on harmony.

13. (a) Emphasizing the chairs with contrast implies that that person receives visitors and is more effective than the other option for emphasis—the desk lamp. Working with their backs to the "action" may be uncomfortable for clerks and may be subtly rude to patrons. Signs and ropes are remedies for a failure to design properly in the first place.

14. (c) Unity that implies movement (such as banners hung in a row) creates rhythm.

15. (b) While balance is important, symmetrical balance is not sought. Contortion is often employed in an effort to create visual movement, but the goals are asymmetry and movement; other options are a means to an end.

16. (c) To deliver traffic to the exhibit naturally and to call attention to it will be more effective than emphasis caused by surrounding materials alone, and pulling it out of context of other similar topics will create confusion. A banner at the ticket booth may be too disassociated with the display to have as much impact.

17. (a) Dynamism implies visual movement, which is most easily created by diagonal lines because lines imply movement and diagonals are perceived as dynamic. Radial balance creates stability at the center and a rhythm, which also causes a perceived movement but is not as emphatic as a line. Multiple focal points will create more confusion than movement.

18. (b) Vertical lines will emphasize height; diminishing the width as vertical elements move away from the viewer will exaggerate the sense of height with this trompe l'oeil effect. A skylight will call attention to the height but will not contribute to an enhanced perception of verticality. Horizontal stripes will diminish the sense of verticality.

Human Factors

19. (a) Because different users will occupy the same chair, it must be adjustable to suit each user.

20. (c) Choices a and b would come from code data; anthropometric data refers to body measurements, which has very little to do with material selections.

21. (b) Warm hues can impact perception of warmth, but actual warmth would be best delivered by heat. If your feet and seat are warm, you will be warmer even if air temperatures are cooler; this will be more noticeable than the heat delivered by incandescent lighting. Do not block the sun in the winter and thereby lose thermal gain from daylight.

22. (c) The keyboard is more comfortable slightly below standard desk height of 30 inches.

23. (d) Worker satisfaction is directly tied to being able to manipulate the environment to suit the individual—which is the flexibility offered by choice d.

24. (c) A widely accepted rule of thumb indicates 30 to 36 inches.

25. (a) People are within social distance, so they must be visually screened to avoid feeling as if they are in each other's space.

26. (c) Creating a sense of ownership will encourage tenants to feel responsible for the corridor. Personalizing their entrances will empower them and foster a sense of ownership out into the corridor.

27. (d) Preferred negotiation position is face-to-face.

28. (c) Choice c pertains to layouts, which are not investigated until after the programming is complete.

29. (b) Choice b is the most specific in terms of needs to be fulfilled without narrowing options by suggesting a solution.

30. (d) The goal of programming is to end up with a program statement of the problem. The other three choices cannot take place until the design has at least been partially implemented—which is well beyond the end of programming.

31. (a) Both the program and the concept include procedural and aesthetic components, and they work together to guide the solution.

32. (c) All but option c can be calculated from plans and specs, but the contribution of users to noise can only be measured when the space is in use.

33. (b) The restrooms do not have as direct an impact on the configuration of the shop as the other issues.

34. (c) Circulation routes, furnished areas, and structural columns are included in area calculations.

35. (c)

6 LF of files can go under the work surface. The space can be 10' x 5' = 50 SF

36. (a) Clients may have requested adjacencies based on previous arrangements and not on real need so, before investing time in rerouting procedures, confirm that requested adjacencies are really necessary. The meeting with the client could also help establish a hierarchy of relationships to determine which are most critical instead of choice b where the designer might not make the best decisions. While it is appropriate to interview users for more info, it is the designer's job to solve the problem.

Space Planning

37. (b) Motorized vehicles require more aisle width than walking humans, so the wider width would override anthropometric data.

38. (a) Landmark status is not likely to impose many restrictions on the kitchen area—same for millwork and chandeliers. Plumbing can be rerouted but structural elements will be more immovable, and existing fenestration is likely to be retained in a landmark building.

39. (b) Option b will not require that the occupant reorient themselves for frequent small meetings.

40. (b) Because this kind of architecture is typically rectilinear, choice b is indicated (eliminating radial, which is the other center orientation).

41. (d) a and b are configurations, not circulation options. Because buildings are typically rectilinear versus round or linear, choices a, b, and c are eliminated. The answer is d.

42. (c) The presumption is that when a space is reconfigured, services will be routed and adjusted as necessary, but structural systems are more difficult to alter.

43. (b) There will be few truly noisy activities at an eye surgeon's offices, but other distinctions are important.

44. (a) Defined in codes

45. (c) Defined in codes

Cost Estimating

46. (c) 6,000 × .6 = 3,600 net × 1.3 = $4,680.

47. (c) (12 × 50) × 1.15 = $690

48. (b) The client will save themselves the contractor's markup. Options a, c, and d could happen even if the appliances were purchased on the contractor's account, so b provides the most significant incentive.

49. (d) The furniture is sold through a dealer who would calculate price, so between the dealer and the designer (who specifies the furniture), the most accurate pricing will be calculated.

50. (c) The general contractor is most familiar with the current pricing structures and is also in a position to discuss expectations and priorities with the designer and to draw up estimates based on location, scope of work, and expectations.

51. (a) 48 in. × 1.3 (stackback) × 2.5 (fullness) = 156 + 24 (hems, overlap, and returns) = 180/48 in. (width of goods) = 3.75 means 4 full panels. Each panel is 84 + 18 = 102 × 4 panels = 408 in. / 36 = 11.3 yd.

52. (b) Calculate the exact quantity needed for the most accurate estimates

53. (d) It is best to find a solution that does not compromise quality. It is not always possible for the client to come up with more money for a project, and designers should always work to meet budget requirements without compromise to quality.

54. (b) The doors are narrower than the wall covering, so wall-covering panels will still be needed at door locations (the door locations are not material to the estimate): 112 LF/54 in. wide goods = 25 panels of wall covering at 120 in. each panel = 83.3333 yd. × $12 = $1,010.

Construction Drawings

55. (c) Locations of walls will be shown most completely on plan views; floor plan views will show partial-height walls, and ceiling plans will show full-height walls.

56. (d) Drafting conventions

57. (a) Individual trades will be responsible for locations of their work but not necessarily each other's work. The general contractor is primarily responsible for orchestrating the work, not defining it.

58. (b) The fit between the cabinet and the building is controlled by levelers and scribes. Because a cabinet that must be leveled will also need scribes, the scribe is the most important insurance for a good fit of cabinet to architecture.

59. (d) Blueprint matching requires that the substrate be cut before the veneer is applied, so complete control over the grain presentation is available with blueprint matching.

60. (c) Layers are concrete slab, sound mat, substrate, and flooring.

61. (b) Stated in ADA codes

62. (a) Stated in ADA codes

63. (d) Solid wood is shown but not enough information is given to presume b or c.

Construction Specifications

64. (c) Loads are defined in anchorage devices, which is the performance descriptor asked about. Other options are material specifications.

65. (a) Because finishes change over time, the finish's exact formulation will not account for the age of the finish. The best way to compensate for this changing with time is to create a visual match between the new and existing finish.

66. (d) Omitting info or using vague terminology is not a good way to make specs more succinct. Referencing standards saves loading a lot of descriptors into your written spec.

67. (c) Any alternatives proposed by the contractor must be approved by the client or designer (depending on the contract) before substituting for the written specs.

68. (b) A proprietary spec identifies the exact product; other answer choices leave room for error or interpretation.

69. (d) Answer a (nonaction) is always risky; answers b and c may be possibilities, but the client should identify priorities with the designer.

70. (a) Answer a is important to design development, and the project manual is primarily for project management.

71. (d) Your verbal communication during the walk-through supplements your clear written instructions; N, S, E, W will not be clear enough for an irregularly shaped office. The best way to communicate this is with clear finish plans.

72. (c) The build-out agreement already precludes options a and b, and option d will not contribute to the installation. Since a separate paperhanger will be hired, they should size the walls too.

Section II: Contract Development and Administration

Contract Documents

73. (d) These are all contract documents and part of a legal contract.

74. (b) An estimate is distinct from a contract; until an estimate becomes a contract, it is not legally binding on anyone.

75. (c) By the implementation phase, the designer has already specified furnishings and finishes, and the general contractor is responsible for coordination of trades; therefore, the only thing to do at this stage is answer c.

76. (b) Legally and contractually, the general contractor is the first person responsible even though anyone may call attention to unsafe conditions.

77. (d) The finish plan pertains to finishes, and the finish plan instructs the painter and paperhanger. Other trades refer to the finish plan in the normal course of their work but not the other three listed.

78. (a) Plan sets are arranged in a hierarchy with broad info followed by specific info. The overall identification and organization of the set is clarified; then plans precede details throughout the set.

79. (d) The spec is referencing data found in another document and is a reference spec.

80. (b) Commonly understood to mean b, unless identified as meaning something different

81. (c) Approval of the drawings defines the next step in the contract; disapproving them later is a change to the work as ordered.

Furniture Fixtures and Equipment

82. (b) The wool/nylon blend will be the most durable, flame and stain resistant.

83. (d) Some of the tests listed are actually measures of sound (NRC and SRC) and pressure (PSI), which the student should recognize. Abrasion resistance and resistance to fading will be important in this space.

84. (a) In this setting, durability will be the most important, and cost is also critical for institutional settings, so design decisions will be made with the first two priorities in mind. Design details would not precede comfort so b is not the best answer; in a hierarchy, finish is minor compared to cost and design, and in option d washability and finish are probably synonymous.

85. (a) Rayon will have the least resistance to fading.

86. (d) The best appearance retention with little maintenance will be provided by foams, and high-density foam will perform the best. This is not a couch-potato scenario indicating a soft "nest," and since the elderly are likely to be in the care of an eye doctor, the firm padding will make it easier for them to get out of the furniture unassisted.

87. (c) Hospitals have the most vulnerable population so you should expect the most stringent codes.

88. (b) Classification A defines flammability.

89. (d) The padding and fabric are the first parts of the construction in contact with a source of ignition, and the two combined contribute to flammability.

90. (a) Good construction practices for durability indicate dovetailed construction for resisting the stresses a drawer endures; a 35-pound particle board is not durable enough for furniture (floor underlayment) and low-pressure laminate is not as abrasion-resistant as high-pressure laminate. This is a high-use/abuse situation best served by option a.

Interior Construction

91. (d) A mortise lock is the most secure of those listed. A card reader activates a lock and may also be called for, but we don't have any info here indicating that is the case.

92. (c) This is a symbol for a metal stud 2 × 4, and it has only one layer of wallboard indicated.

93. (a) It is a construction that students should have encountered as meeting a 1-hour requirement.

94. (b) Rift provides straight grain, which is not obscured by the cross-banding of quarter sawn.

95. (c) All choices except for c contribute to the door's ability to provide privacy.

96. (c) Interior designers are not qualified to make a judgment in cases of load-bearing, and other experts must be responsible for that. Plans may not reflect actual conditions so the safest thing to do is have the site inspected by a qualified professional.

97. (d) The danger of a person mistaking option d for an opening are reduced sufficiently for most codes to allow regular glass in this instance.

Finishes

98. (b) Peelable leaves a nice substrate for future paper installations, and the client will not have to have the paper steamed off the wall.

99. (b) Type III is the most durable option.

100. (c) The solid, flat, yet slip-resistant surface of the flamed granite will be easier for maintenance than travertine or river rock.

101. (d) This is the most common flooring installed and is presumed unless something else is described.

102. (b) The most even installation will be the thickset. Random slate must have wide grout joints, eliminating unsanded grout; cork is not rigid enough for a material with no give, and dry-fit refers to a step during installation and not to an installation method.

103. (c) Sheet vinyl and sheet rubber would be the easiest to maintain, but rubber is degraded by oils, which are frequently used in kitchens.

104. (c) Corridors have a lot of wheeled traffic and stretched-in carpet is too likely to move under wheeled traffic.

105. (d) Grout release is used as its name implies.

106. (b) Options a and c will make the surfaces different from each other at the outset, and closed pore with filler will not really make a difference. However, option b brings consistency to the installation and protects it from changing differently over time due to light because it has UV protection.

Lighting

107. (c) Because color comparisons are so important, the ability of the lighting to render color accurately is the most crucial characteristic here.

108. (a) Sparkle is the most important contribution to crystal displays.

109. (d) Glossy paper's shiny surface will reflect light, causing veiling reflections.

110. (c) Indirect ambient light will create less glare on computer screens, and being able to adjust light angles from a task light on the desk will avoid glare and control light levels for paper tasks.

111. (b) The best display of merchandise is so dependant on the quality of the light that we can't assume that we will have a successful scheme by providing less light or by switching to fluorescent lighting; however, we do need more efficient lamps that won't have to be replaced. The best first step is to find more efficient lamps.

112. (d) Electrical contractors install equipment according to plans by electrical engineers. Interior designers specify type and location of equipment, but the design of the entire system would be the responsibility of the electrical engineer on a large commercial job.

113. (b) Balance the daylight at the window with the lighting in the deep interior so the table area doesn't seem underlit by comparison. Simply using bright light at night will not take care of this, and choice c is, frankly, goofy.

114. (a) To maximize texture, graze the surface. Because the corridor width is narrow, uplighting will cause direct glare (people will have to walk close to the light and will see the light source).

115. (c) Choice c maximizes contrast between risers and treads so the changing surfaces are easy to distinguish and the stairs will be safer.

Mechanical and Electrical Systems

116. (d) Wood is combustible, and the communication required for using the plenum as a return also allows flame to spread to wood and would be prohibited.

117. (c) Matter of fact

118. (d) The continued safety and performance of the glass and the effect on heating loads are material to health and safety. The building owner will approve the material in light of these and appearance issues. The new covering will affect the lighting issues, but they are less critical and alterable to some extent with lamping changes.

119. (b) It is understood to be an exit light unless the legend states otherwise.

120. (d) Seven-inch risers deliver an even number, and 7/11 is often used as a starting point for calculating numbers of risers and run of stairs. 116 + 10 = 126 in./7 = 18 risers even. Since the 7-inch riser fits perfectly use the suggested 7/11.

121. (a) These shelving units are very heavy, and support must be evaluated.

122. (b) Convector units are shared between spaces, and sound can easily travel through them.

123. (a) Access floors are designed to run electrical and communication conduits, so they would not be the prohibited elements. Plumbing pipe is part of the building and must be installed per code, so water pipes would be prohibited.

124. (b) The danger is flame being drawn along air passage routes, so the solution is a fire damper that screens this passage of flame but allows air to move (unlike obstructions and insulation). Combustion in the plenum is secondary to flames being drawn through it.

Acoustics

125. (d) The most precise answer is d—it could be argued that it is accomplished by means such as those posed in option b, but it is not strictly a sound baffle.

126. (b) Impact sound telegraphing through materials and airborne sound are the two ways that sound migrates into other spaces, so the need to control transmission through air and materials makes b the best answer.

127. (a) Acoustical tiles absorb and fracture sound waves, reducing the sound that bounces off and returns to the space (reverberation).

128. (c) Even a small surface can effectively transmit sound.

129. (c) You want to deliver sound clearly, and oblique angles will break up the sound.

130. (b) A few decibels' difference is imperceptible, and 7 is considered the difference that is noticeable. Good acoustical materials control for the preferred presentation, which usually diminishes some kinds of sounds over others. Live surfaces are included in designs to deliver sound undistorted, and elimination of all background noise is usually undesirable, because this will create an anechoic effect that people find disturbing.

131. (d) Even the smallest direct line allows sound through. Location dependent solution requires no *special materials,* as included in other answer choices.

132. (a) It covers existing sound (of conversations) and can be monotonous, as it imitates the hum of equipment. It is usually employed to limit speech intelligibility from one space to another.

133. (b) The best answer is b, because it is more precise; option a could be selected too, but it is vague and does not distinguish what is really happening. Options c and d would not be accomplished by insulation in the wall.

Communication Methods

134. (d) Matter of fact

135. (b) All lines converging on the vanishing point is a device often used to direct attention to that portion of the drawing.

136. (a) They illustrate a view as we are used to seeing it. They aren't the best options for portraying organization of space (plan view) or scale (elevation or isometric), and only one view is available in the drawing.

137. (d) Plan views are "bird's-eye" views.

138. (c) The drafting convention most typically employed uses line weight to visually strengthen items that stand in front of other items so they visually pop away from their backgrounds or to call attention to important elements of the drawing.

139. (a) Perspective drawings would also require vanishing points above and below the horizon for accuracy. One- and two-point perspectives are usually adjusted to suit the renderer's eye to handle the distortion that occurs if the drawing was constructed without these additional vanishing points.

140. (b) A vertical section is an elevation showing multiple levels otherwise unseen. Measured drawings, even if 3-D, serve a different purpose than perspectives.

141. (c) Grids can be applied to other drawings listed, but the grid is integral to the accuracy of the perspective.

142. (a) Relative scale may be available in the plan view, but proportions are better shown in to-scale elevations, so a is the least true.

143. (d) The perspective simulates a view as we would see it if it existed to be seen. Furniture and materials are best illustrated with photos and samples, and construction details are better shown as isometrics if a 3-D view is preferable to a 2-D view.

Building Codes

144. (b) Students should be able to distinguish between service and selling classifications for occupancy; this building is masonry (brick) and heavy timber construction and, anything over four stories is considered a high-rise.

145. (c) Exit enclosures are required to protect people exiting in the case of a fire in the building, so flame-spread ratings are more stringent in these areas regardless of the other classifications by which the building is defined.

146. (d) Testing the entire construction, not just the materials in isolation, will provide the most realistic evaluation.

147. (a) Allowable occupancy numbers will best define the number of fixtures regardless of space required to meet accessibility. Building type does not impact the best number as much as difficulty in providing it. While a grandfather clause may allow a location to fall outside recommendations, designers should always design to provide for recommended numbers of fixtures.

148. (c) Refer to an occupancy group to determine what the rating should be and where materials of various ratings may be used.

149. (a) Matter of fact

150. (d) Wire obstructs the clarity of the partition, and ballistic glass is overkill for the description provided.

Exiting

151. (b) Matter of fact

152. (d) Kitchens are considered to be hazardous areas and may not be used as part of an exit route.

153. (a) Required width cannot be reduced by door swings, so it would be width *plus* door swings; they must be accessible, and they can be used for normal use circulation too. They must comply with fire ratings assigned.

154. (b) Matter of fact

155. (c) 7 SF per person for dance floor = 142, dining room = 266, kitchen = 5, and bar = 66 = 479.

156. (d) Matter of fact

157. (a) This information is essential to looking up the distance limitations in code books.

158. (b) Options a and d do not play a role in calculating the number of exits, and classification will be accounted for but is impacted by number of people using the space.

159. (a) The number of people moving through the corridor has a direct impact on the required width.

Barrier Free

160. (d) Defined by ADA (Americans with Disabilities Act)

161. (b) Defined by ADA

162. (c) Defined by ADA

163. (a) Pedestal, freestanding, and vanities all present obstructions that are not present with wall-hung sinks.

164. (b) Defined by ADA

165. (d) Option d will best protect the widest range of people.

166. (a) A few possible approaches may be used, so these should be considered in space planning. The door swing delivers the user in a convenient or inconvenient way, which is why option a is critical. Grab-bar height is not critical to space planning. Options c and d are considerations contained in option a.

167. (b) Options a, c, and d include dimensions above and below the most comfortable range.

168. (d) Option d allows you to avoid violating code, avoid the unnecessary expense of making changes to the building envelope, and avoid the inconvenience for users.

Owner-Designer Agreements

169. (a) Options b, c, and d are all part of the cost of doing the work contracted for. Copying expense is not part of the design work and is usually reimbursable.

170. (b) Sometimes clients do not understand that these requests will impact cost and completion, so first get in touch with the client to understand what is driving the request and what the impact will be. Only after this conversation can you communicate with others and plan for the changes required.

171. (c) The contractor building the niche has no reason to refer to the furnishings page; the complete info for constructing the niche is presumed to be on the partition plan. The error is the designer's, even if the partition drawings could be interpreted in more than one way.

172. (d) If you are efficient and bring the job in under the hourly estimate, you are penalized by lower fees. If you exceed the initial estimate, you work for free after you reach the estimate.

173. (b) Options a and d are requests for funds to be released; the bill of lading documents transport. It is the PO that accompanies the release of funds for a furniture purchase.

174. (a) These are commonly described in the contract between the owner and the designer.

175. (b) Options c and d are illegal; the most direct way to solve the problem is to use the services of a structural engineer (architects often hire them as well as designers). Because there is little architectural planning required, an architect is more service than is needed.

176. (d) The owner is ultimately responsible for the project and hires professionals to help, so a, b, and c are true. Option d is not true, because the termination of the project can be negotiated at any time, and the design work is easily separated from implementing the design.

Professional Practice

177. (c) Errors and omissions insurance is carried only by design professionals. The other insurance types would be a matter of contract dependant on the specific project.

178. (a) The partnership exists only in the founders.

179. (b) The furniture dealer is responsible for delivering acceptable merchandise, which is determined at the time of inspection. The remedies they seek from others are independent of this responsibility.

180. (d) Options a, b, and c cover this condition. The individual's health insurance may come into play in case of an accident, but if it does not exist, the employer's liability is covered by the first three options.

181. (a) Marketing and PR do not supply goods and services needed to do business.

182. (c) Although option d is likely, the designer is better off if the purchases remain with the client; options a and b may be employed as the designer attempts to accomplish option c.

183. (b) It is a bad idea to enter into a contract that is in conflict with another contract; therefore, the relationship with the first designer should be formally ended. The collaboration with the other designer is likely to be uncomfortable for everyone. Since you are a designer with an interest and not a mediator, you should not step into that role.

184. (a) More pointed efforts such as the brochure that you distribute where it is logical are better than expensive ads and scattershot mailings. Stationery is not a marketing plan.

185. (d) They are not the easiest to set up (sole proprietorship is).

Project Coordination

186. (c) The designer is responsible for designing in compliance with the law.

187. (a) The door was ordered from the manufacturer by the general contractor, and the opening was framed under the general contractor's contract.

188. (d) The POE evaluates the success of the current project.

189. (b) Options a, c, and d are implicit in the furniture contract as the responsibility of the furniture contractor, but option b can only be provided by the client.

190. (c) The person who sells the goods to the client is responsible for the order.

191. (d) Option d is the responsibility of the design staff, not management.

192. (b) The client should be made aware of the safety issue, and it may be important later to have some documentation of the issue on record. Immediately bring it to the attention of the general contractor so it can be rectified before someone gets hurt.

193. (a) Confirming that the work is in compliance with specs is the primary responsibility of the designer. Just checking on the work (option b) is too passive. How the work is completed is not the domain of the designer—the outcome of the work is.

194. (c) Items must be turned over in acceptable condition, and minor touch-ups may be required to allow for that. The repair of anything too major to be handled on-site will be orchestrated by the seller.

195. (b) While all the above may come into play, the designer is the one to clarify the meaning of their drawings and specs.

196. (c) All except option c are reasons to withhold approval payment if the work is "substantially complete."

MULTIPLE-CHOICE EXAM

Lite Version

SECTION I

Principles and Practices of Interior Design, Lite Version

This Lite version of the Interior Design exam imitates the scope but not the scale of the exam. The multiple-choice answers are listed at the back of the study guide, and provide an explanation for the instructor as to why the answer is correct.

Elements and Principles of Design

1. A stucco wall is one way to create

   a. pattern.
   b. texture.
   c. line.
   d. color.

2. In order to maximize safety and visibility on stairs,

   a. install a carpet with a large pattern as a runner secured with carpet rods.
   b. use a different material on each tread.
   c. highlight the treads and cast the risers in shadow.
   d. install a halogen wall sconce above each tread location.

3. The greatest contrast will be created from

   a. two shades of varying temperature.
   b. two saturated complementary colors.
   c. two tints of varying temperature.
   d. an analogous pair of colors.

4. To create visual unity between a spindled staircase and the surrounding space,

   a. use a wallpaper with vertical stripes.
   b. use a foliate-patterned wall covering in a contrasting color.
   c. employ horizontal stripes across from the stairs.
   d. paint the risers to match the treads.

5. To emphasize the location of the check-in desk of an elegant, traditional hotel,

   a. inset arrows of an expensive, elegant flooring material to direct patrons to the desk.
   b. use a startling, asymmetrical balance to attract attention to the desk.
   c. position sound system speakers over the desk and employ music to call attention to desk location.
   d. use increased light levels at desk and symmetrical balance left and right with the desk in the center.

6. Harmony in a spa setting would be *most* reliant on

   a. proportion.
   b. unity.
   c. scale.
   d. color schemes.

7. Hanging regularly spaced, similar banners along the pedestrian corridor of a strip mall would be most effective in creating

   a. proportion.
   b. variety.
   c. rhythm.
   d. balance.

8. To create a dynamic presentation of space, a designer would employ

   a. diagonal lines.
   b. radial balance.
   c. repetition creating rhythm.
   d. multiple focal points.

9. To enhance the impression of height within a space,

   a. gradually shift the color from cool near the floor to warm near the top.
   b. employ vertical elements that diminish in width as they extend upward.
   c. install a skylight.
   d. employ horizontal stripes near the floor that stop before reaching eye level, and paint the wall above in a cool color.

Human Factors

10. The most important feature of an ergonomically correct chair for the teller of a 24-hour currency exchange would be

    a. adjustability.
    b. lumbar support.
    c. tilt and swivel.
    d. firm cushioning.

11. The designer is likely to use anthropometric data to determine

    a. the allowable projection of a wall sconce in a public corridor.
    b. the width of an exit corridor.
    c. the height and depth of a transaction surface.
    d. the durability of a surfacing material.

12. The ideal height of a keyboard for a computer is

    a. 30 to 32¾ inches.
    b. 28½ to 32¾ inches.
    c. 26 to 28½ inches.
    d. 18 to 24 inches.

13. The minimum clear distance from the edge of a table to an obstruction that allows for a user to push back their chair and rise away from a table is

    a. 18 to 24 inches.
    b. 24 to 30 inches.
    c. 30 to 36 inches.
    d. 36 to 40 inches.

14. When arranging study carrels in a public library, mitigate the problem of proximity by

    a. clearly demarcating territory with an enclosure that screens view.
    b. using neutral materials.
    c. using a light-reflecting material on sides of carrel.
    d. selecting durable, easily maintained surfacing material.

Programming

15. The following is *not* part of the programming process:

    a. Establish goals both stated and unstated
    b. Establish which areas of code impact solution
    c. Establish private zones within the footprint
    d. Establish user requirements

16. The last step in the programming phase is

    a. post occupancy evaluation.
    b. user survey.
    c. site inspection.
    d. statement of the problem.

17. If you were conducting a programming interview for a souvenir shop, which of the following is *least* important?

    a. Which items are most often purchased on "impulse"
    b. Location of the restrooms
    c. Typical size and type of items for sale
    d. Security needs

18. The adjacency matrix has identified several *requested* adjacencies that cannot all be satisfied within the building footprint. Your best course of action is to

    a. confirm that the adjacencies identified all require physical connection by reviewing the situation with client.
    b. prioritize based on research and solve for maximizing required connections.
    c. identify in specifications one or more alternative routing systems and info-sharing options to eliminate adjacency needs that can't be met by space planning.
    d. interview users for suggestions.

Space Planning

19. After the approved block plan of a hotel renovation has established the area to be allocated to the restaurant and kitchen, which of the following has the *most* influence over the planning of the area?

    a. Existing structural columns and structural walls, windows and exit locations
    b. Whether or not the building has landmark status
    c. Locations of existing plumbing
    d. Existing ornate millwork and chandeliers

20. Of the following open office layouts below, which is *most* convenient for a project manager who has numerous staff consultations throughout the day?

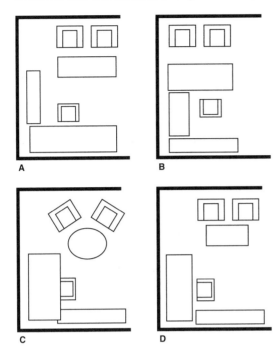

21. Dead-end corridors in an office building should not exceed how many feet in length?

a. 20 feet
b. 30 feet
c. 40 feet
d. 50 feet

22. Plans for the expansion of a restaurant require an additional exit. Your primary concern for its location is to

a. minimize its appearance so patrons do not confuse it with the front door.
b. ensure that it does not open into an alleyway or onto private property.
c. keep the location as remote as possible from the existing entrance.
d. position it as close to the entrance as possible so that patrons are familiar with it so they can find it easily.

Cost Estimating

23. A credenza that lists for $6,000 and is a 40 percent-off item that a designer sells at net plus 30 percent would cost the client before freight, taxes, and delivery

a. $3,120.
b. $2,520.
c. $4,680.
d. $7,384.

24. If the standard rule of thumb in your area is that a drywall partition costs about $50 per lineal foot regardless of height, and contractors typically charge a 15 percent markup, what will you estimate your client's 12-foot long × 8-foot tall partition wall will cost?

a. $90
b. $690
c. $720
d. $1,350

25 The most accurate budget figures for a furnishing job can be drawn up by the

a. furniture manufacturer and interior designer.
b. general contractor and interior designer.
c. furniture manufacturer and client.
d. interior designer and furniture dealer.

26. Which method of estimating would provide the *most* accurate quantity projection?

a. Square footage
b. Quantity takeoff
c. Rule of thumb
d. Estimating chart

Construction Drawings

27. The location of slab-to-slab partitions dividing a space are most clearly shown on which of the following?

a. Interior elevations
b. Interior wall sections
c. Reflected ceiling plans
d. Finish plans

28. The above symbol indicates

    a. a building section.
    b. the location of an interior section in the document set.
    c. a detail drawing indicator.
    d. the existence of an elevation view.

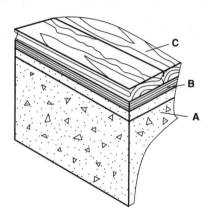

The next four questions relate to the above diagram.

29. In the above diagram, "A" represents

    a. sound-deadening material.
    b. concrete slab.
    c. original terrazzo floor with new surface adhered.
    d. thickset.

30. In the above diagram, "C" illustrates

    a. engineered flooring product.
    b. rift-sawn wood.
    c. plain-sawn oak.
    d. dimensional wood strip flooring.

Construction Specifications

31. Which item in the following specification excerpt is a performance specification?

Part 2 Products
   2.01 Metal Support material
   General: to the extent not otherwise indicated, comply with ASTM C754 for metal system supporting gypsum wallboard
   Ceiling suspension main runners: 1-1/2-inch steel channels, cold rolled
   Hanger wire: ASTM A641, soft, Class 1 galvanized pre-stretched, sized in accordance with ASTM C754
   Hanger anchorage devices: size for 3 times calculated loads, except size direct-pull concrete inserts for 5 times calculated loads
   Studs: ASTM C645; 25 gauge, 2-1/2 inches deep, except as otherwise indicated
   Runners: Match studs; type recommended by stud manufacturer for vertical abutment of drywall work at other work

   a. Ceiling suspension main runners
   b. Hanger wire
   c. Hanger anchorage devices
   d. Hanger wire

32. What does the term "approved equal" mean when it appears in a specification?

    a. The client and designer must both agree upon the specification.
    b. The contractor may substitute any product with similar specifications.
    c. A specification has been given, but the contractor may submit alternatives for approval.
    d. The client and the designer have reserved the right to change the specification after the work has begun.

33. What is the best way to ensure that the exact product you want will be installed?

    a. Write a descriptive specification including performance requirements
    b. Write a proprietary specification including all manufacturers' ID numbers
    c. Require that material be returnable at designer's discretion
    d. Include a picture of the item in schedules prepared for bid

34. You are specifying multiple wall finishes to be used in an irregularly-shaped office. The best way to convey the information so the correct finish material is used on each surface is

    a. conducting an on-site walk-through with the painting contractor and using verbal instructions.
    b. designating N, S, E, W, on the finish schedule.
    c. specifying your office as the ship-to location so the material cannot be installed until you have reviewed location with installers.
    d. using a combination of lines and symbols on plans and elevations to show clearly in the document set where each material is to be used.

SECTION II

Contract Development and Administration

Contract Documents

35. Which of the following are legal documents?

    a. Specifications
    b. Schedules
    c. Drawings
    d. All of the above

36. During the contract administration (implementation) phase of a project, the designer is responsible for

    a. furniture specifications.
    b. coordination of trades.
    c. meeting with the general contractor and conducting site visits.
    d. finish specifications.

37. The finish plan will be used by the

    a. carpenter.
    b. electrician.
    c. furniture installer.
    d. painter/paperhanger.

38. In a typical set of construction drawings, sheets will be ordered as follows:

    a. Title and index page, then floor plans, then reflected ceiling plans
    b. Floor plans, then details, then elevations all indexed at the end
    c. Title and index page, then details, then elevations
    d. Floor plans, then electrical plan, then elevations

39. NIC means

    a. no interior contract.
    b. not in contract.
    c. not in compliance.
    d. not intended for construction.

Furniture Fixtures and Equipment

40. Which of the following would you specify for upholstery in a family-style restaurant?

    a. Silk/wool blend
    b. Wool/nylon blend
    c. Cotton/rayon blend
    d. Acrylic/acetate blend

41. What performance tests should you specify for fabric used in the multipurpose room of a community center?

    a. Double-rubs and NRC
    b. Indentation load deflection and SRC
    c. PSI and Fade-Ometer
    d. Wyzenbeeck and fading

42. Which of the following should you be *least* likely to specify for a sunroom sofa?

    a. Rayon
    b. Polyester
    c. Modacrylic
    d. Acrylic

43. Class A fabric will not

    a. rot.
    b. ignite.
    c. char.
    d. smolder.

Interior Construction

The next two questions relate to the following diagram.

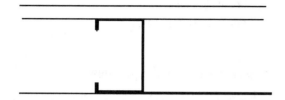

44. What type of partition is indicated by the above diagram?

    a. 3½-inch wooden stud with ⅝-inch gypsum wallboard
    b. 1½-inch metal stud with two layers of ½-inch gypsum wallboard
    c. 3⅝-inch metal stud with ⅝-inch gypsum wallboard
    d. 3½-inch wooden stud with wood paneling

45. It has a fire rating of

    a. 1 hour.
    b. 2 hour.
    c. 4 hour.
    d. It is not suitable for a rated partition.

46. If a client wanted to remove a partition that may be a load-bearing wall, what is your best course of action?

    a. Send a letter to the building department in that jurisdiction so they can adjust their records relative to that building
    b. Review original building plans to confirm the wall's purpose
    c. Have an engineer or architect review the problem and make a recommendation
    d. Look in the attic to determine what loads are being borne by the partition

47. Safety glazing is likely not required in which of the following locations?

    a. Glass serving as railing on a staircase
    b. Shower doors
    c. Full-height glass sidelights next to a solid wood door
    d. Sidelights in a residential door unit where the sill is greater than 18 inches AFF

Finishes

48. In order to allow your client to easily change the wallpaper above the chair rail in her dining room, you would specify

    a. pre-pasted.
    b. peelable.
    c. Type II vinyl.
    d. laminated paper.

49. The most functional floor for the entrance to a nature preserve's education center would be

    a. unfilled travertine.
    b. polished granite.
    c. granite with a flamed finish.
    d. mesh-mounted river rock in mortar.

50. Your design firm is coordinating surfacing selections with the architect's details. You have in mind to use an ungauged, cleft-face slate floor over concrete slab in a client's sun room. Which installation method will be most successful?

    a. ½-inch thick mortar bed to prevent cracks with dry-set stone on top
    b. Thickset with a cleavage membrane under the stone to prevent cracks
    c. Thin-set installation with unsanded grout
    d. Floating floor installation with ½-inch cork underlayment

51. You are carefully matching wood finishes throughout a space. In order to ensure that the appearance remains as consistent as possible over time, you will do the following:

    a. Specify a variety of gloss levels and tint the sealant or stain the wood
    b. Consistently use solids or veneers of the same species with the same formulation with UV protection for sealant
    c. Use a lacquer finish on some items so there is less wood, and seal with a sealant with UV protection
    d. Use a closed pore finish with filler matched from one surface to the next

Lighting

52. What is the most important criterion when specifying lighting for a fabric showroom?

    a. Color temperature
    b. Visual comfort
    c. Color rendering index
    d. Coefficient of utilization

53. The best light source for highlighting the crystal in a department store would be

   a. 75-watt MR-16 for sparkle.
   b. incandescent A-19 for ease of maintenance.
   c. cool-white deluxe fluorescent for economy.
   d. metal halide for brightness.

54. It is quite common for office tasks to combine review of printed material with work at the computer. Which of the following would be the most appropriate approach to lighting the space?

   a. Direct/indirect controlled at each station
   b. Low-brightness troffers on dimmer switches and a task light at each station
   c. Indirect ambient light with an adjustable task light at each station
   d. Adjustable downlights over desks and indirect light on each terminal

55. Who would be responsible for the installation details of computerized control equipment, circuitry, and light fixture installation details for a large commercial installation?

   a. Electrical contractor
   b. Interior designer
   c. General contractor
   d. Electrical engineer

56. When lighting stairs, it is most important to provide

   a. 100-foot lamberts on treads.
   b. 100 foot-candles on treads.
   c. contrast between risers and treads.
   d. indirect lighting on risers.

Mechanical and Electrical Systems

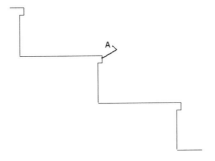

57. In the above diagram, "A" is indicating the

   a. stringer.
   b. riser.
   c. nosing.
   d. toe clip.

58. The above symbol indicates

   a. recessed floor data line.
   b. ceiling-suspended exit light.
   c. wall washer or adjustable light fixture.
   d. emergency lighting.

59. Which of the following would be prohibited under the panels of an access floor in an office for a stock-trading company?

   a. Plumbing pipe
   b. Electrical conduit
   c. Computer cable
   d. Low-voltage wire

60. In a plenum ceiling space, which handles air for the HVAC system, how would you prevent a fire from spreading horizontally?

   a. Pack the plenum with fiberglass insulation
   b. Bolt a fire damper to the underside of the floor slab above
   c. Use a fire-rated panel system and run it up to the upper slab
   d. Install sprinklers above and below the finished ceiling

Acoustics

61. A "floating floor" system with a sound abatement may contribute to sound control in high-rise buildings by

   a. minimizing impact against the floor surface.
   b. creating a sound baffle with insulation.
   c. preventing sound leaks where plumbing pipe penetrates the deck.
   d. preventing sound from telegraphing through materials.

62. In a small performance space, it would be best to avoid

   a. amplifiers.
   b. parallel walls.
   c. numerous oblique angles.
   d. carpeting.

63. White noise is desirable in office situations because

   a. it creates acoustical privacy.
   b. it improves concentration and reduces monotony.
   c. its presence causes users to perceive the space as "elegant."
   d. it masks the hum of electrical equipment.

Communication Methods

64. A drawing that produces a 3-D view that can be measured with a scale ruler at any location in the drawing is considered

   a. an orthographic projection.
   b. a two-point perspective.
   c. an oblique drawing.
   d. isometric.

65. Perspective drawings are the most easily understood by clients because

   a. they are most like the way we perceive space and objects.
   b. they are the fastest way to show the organization of the space.
   c. they are the most accurate in portraying scale.
   d. multiple viewpoints are available within a single drawing.

66. A bird's-eye view is most accurately shown by

   a. a two-point perspective.
   b. an orthographic projection.
   c. an isometric.
   d. a plan view.

67. In a line drawing, a hierarchy of information can be conveyed by

   a. varying the level of detail so objects in front are more detailed.
   b. varying the value so objects in back are darker.
   c. using a variety of line weights to emphasize important elements.
   d. adding symbols to drawings as an aid to organization.

68. Which of the following is *least* true of drawings?

   a. Proportions of items in a space are best compared in a plan view.
   b. A good drawing answers all questions generated by its existence.
   c. Inserting a human form can help describe scale of a space presented.
   d. One 3-D view is better than two 2-D views to describe the junction between two planes.

Building Codes

69. When referring to the code book for codes pertaining to a loft conversion for a seven-story brick building with wooden posts and flooring systems to be occupied by business tenants providing services, you would refer to

   a. masonry construction, mercantile, and high-rise classifications.
   b. heavy timber and masonry, business, and high-rise classifications.
   c. masonry construction business and low-rise classifications.
   d. fire-resistive, service occupancy, and high-rise classifications.

70. Where are flame-spread ratings most restrictive in all building and occupancy classification types?

   a. In enclosed areas
   b. In unfamiliar locations
   c. In exit enclosures
   d. On corridor floors

Exiting

71. Exits in a restaurant may never pass through

   a. lobbies.
   b. service corridors.
   c. bar areas.
   d. kitchens.

72. Which is the *most* correct statement about exit corridors?

   a. They are calculated as required width plus door swings.
   b. They must be used for only egress.
   c. They must be enclosed by fire-rated partitions.
   d. They need not be accessible.

73. The rise of a stairway means the

   a. distance measured from nosing to nosing.
   b. total of one riser plus two treads.
   c. total of two risers plus one tread.
   d. distance from finished slab to finished slab.

74. You are developing the space planning for a full-floor tenant in a high-rise building. What two things must you know to determine travel distance?

    a. The building type and what the occupancy classification is

    b. Building orientation and whether the building is sprinklered

    c. Height of the building and construction type

    d. Height of the building and whether the building is sprinklered

75. Corridor widths are primarily controlled by

    a. occupancy load.

    b. length of exit travel.

    c. building-use classification.

    d. building-type classification.

Barrier Free

76. The minimum clear floor space required for a wheelchair is

    a. 36 by 40 inches.

    b. 36 by 48 inches.

    c. 30 by 40 inches.

    d. 30 by 48 inches.

77. The minimum depth (not height) required under accessible lavatories is

    a. 12 inches.

    b. 17 inches.

    c. 24 inches.

    d. 28 inches.

78. When designing a hotel that will accommodate the disabled, which of the following would be most important to include?

    a. Visual alarms and flashing smoke detectors

    b. Tactile signage and audible alarms

    c. Audible alarms and large, contrasted lettering on signage

    d. Audible and visual alarms

79. Measured from the nosing to the center of the handrail, which height will meet universal design concepts?

    a. 30 to 38 inches

    b. 34 to 38 inches

    c. 34 to 48 inches

    d. 28 to 45 inches

Owner–Designer Agreements

80. Which of the following is a reimbursable expense?

    a. Copying costs

    b. Producing a study model for space-planning purposes

    c. Extra liability insurance required specifically for the project

    d. A temporary worker to assemble multiple spec books for a meeting

81. The designer specified manufactured case goods for a niche that was built according to the designer's drawings. The dimensions of the case goods are called out on the furnishings page of the document set that was on the site for construction purposes. The case goods do not fit into the niche. Who pays for correcting the problem?

    a. General contractor

    b. Carpentry subcontractor

    c. Designer

    d. Owner

82. Which type of fee is least advantageous to the designer?

    a. Hourly rate

    b. Flat fee

    c. Retail

    d. Hourly with a not-to-exceed cap

83. Which document is used to release funds for the purchase of furniture?

    a. Application for payment

    b. Purchase order

    c. Bill of lading

    d. Final invoice

84. In order to meet all program requirements, a load-bearing partition must be partially removed. The best course of action is

    a. the client hires an architect to draw up the required plans.

    b. the designer or client hires a structural engineer to draw up the plans.

    c. the contractor devises a way to safely modify the partition.

    d. the owner assumes responsibility for the structure, and the work proceeds as drawn by the designer.

Professional Practice

85. Which type of insurance is *not* ultimately the client's responsibility to fund?

    a. Property
    b. Workers' compensation
    c. Errors and omissions
    d. General liability

86. Which of the following is *not* considered a trade resource?

    a. Marketing and PR
    b. Custom fabricator
    c. Furniture showroom
    d. Furniture dealer

87. The most appropriate marketing plan for a new design firm would be

    a. an identity package and brochure with services offered.
    b. stationery and business cards.
    c. print media ads in consumer publications.
    d. direct-mail ad campaign.

88. Which of the following is not true of a corporation?

    a. Generally taxed at a lower rate than individuals
    b. If sued, stockholder assets are not at risk
    c. Might have only one person in the whole corporation
    d. They are the easiest business form to set up

Project Coordination

89. A shop drawing for a custom door is produced by the door manufacturer and was ordered through the general contractor. The interior designer failed to find an error in a dimension stringer. The frame that was produced in accordance with the drawing did not fit the opening that was to receive it. Who is responsible for correcting the mistake?

    a. The general contractor
    b. The interior designer
    c. The framing contractor
    d. The door fabricator

90. Which of the following is not part of the post occupancy evaluation?

    a. Review of the effectiveness of this HVAC system
    b. Interview with representative users of the project
    c. A check on maintenance problems
    d. Suggestions to the client for future projects at the site

91. The furniture contractor can legitimately request which of the following?

    a. Final inspection and acceptance by the owner prior to furniture installation
    b. Extra storage space for furniture that has been delivered to the site
    c. Extra insurance for goods in transit from the warehouse to the site
    d. Additional workers for initial preparation of furniture

92. Which of the following is the *least* important task for the project manager?

    a. Planning weekly use of staff time
    b. Staying current with the client's opinion of how the job is progressing
    c. Keeping notes on all conversations and meeting summaries
    d. Organizing the layout of the construction drawing set

93. During the administration phase of the project, the interior designer is primarily responsible for

    a. confirming the work is in accordance with the contract documents.
    b. checking on the quality and quantity of work.
    c. confirming appropriateness of the means, methods, techniques, and procedures of the work.
    d. acts or omissions of contractors or suppliers carrying out the work.

94. The interior designer may not withhold approval of a payout to a contractor for which of the following:

    a. Reasonable evidence that the work will not be completed on time
    b. Reasonable evidence that the work cannot be completed for the unpaid balance of the contract sum
    c. The punch list hasn't been completed 100 percent
    d. Probability of third-party claims

Lite Version

Elements and Principles of Design

1. (b) Stucco is a plastic material (until it cures), so it is capable of being worked into various textures that can be seen as patterns but are mainly texture.

2. (c) Patterns and color changes may be visually confusing to some users, and a sconce at each tread is excessive. Illuminating treads and contrasting these with shadow on the risers will create the best distinction between risers and treads.

3. (b) Complementary colors will vary in hue and temperature, and often in value as well, so they present the most contrast.

4. (a) Similarity creates unity, and spindles and vertical stripes have the most in common.

5. (d) Arrows in the floor and asymmetrical balance are out of character for an elegant traditional hotel, and speakers would interfere with conversation at the desk. Light is a powerful way to emphasize and will best draw attention to the desk.

6. (b) Harmony is most often described as the perfect balance between unity and variety, so of the options listed, unity has the most impact on harmony.

7 (c) Banners hung in a row will create rhythm.

8. (a) Dynamism implies visual movement, which is most easily created by diagonal lines because lines imply movement and diagonals are perceived as dynamic. Radial balance creates stability at the center and a rhythm, which also causes a perceived movement, is not as emphatic as a line. Multiple focal points will create more confusion than movement.

9. (b) Vertical lines will emphasize height; diminishing the width as vertical elements move away from the viewer will exaggerate the sense of distance with this trompe l'oeil effect. A skylight will call attention to the height but will not contribute to an enhanced perception of verticality. Horizontal stripes will diminish the sense of verticality.

Human Factors

10. (a) Because different users will occupy the same chair, it must be adjustable to suit each user.

11. (c) Choices a and b would come from code data; anthropometric data refers to body measurements, which has very little to do with material selections.

12. (c) The keyboard is more comfortable slightly below standard desk height of 30 inches.

13. (c) A widely accepted rule of thumb indicates 30 to 36 inches.

14. (a) People are within social distance, so they must be visually screened to avoid feeling as if they are in each other's space.

15. (c) Choice c pertains to layouts, which are not investigated until after the programming is complete.

16. (d) The goal of programming is to end up with a program statement of the problem. The other three choices cannot take place until the design has at least been partially implemented—which is well beyond the end of programming.

17. (b) The restrooms do not have as direct an impact on the configuration of the shop as the other issues.

18. (a) Clients may have requested adjacencies based on previous arrangements and not on real need so, before investing time in rerouting procedures, confirm that requested adjacencies are really necessary. The meeting with the client could also help establish a hierarchy of relationships to determine which are most critical instead of choice b where the designer might not make the best decisions. While it is appropriate to interview users for more info, it is the designer's job to solve the problem.

Space Planning

19. (a) Landmark status is not likely to impose many restrictions on the kitchen area—same for millwork and chandeliers. Plumbing can be rerouted but structural elements will be more immovable, and existing fenestration is likely to be retained in a landmark building.

20. (b) Option b will not require that the occupant reorient themselves for frequent small meetings.

21. (a) Defined in codes

22. (c) Defined in codes

Cost Estimating

23. (c) $6,000 \times .6 = 3,600$ net $\times 1.3 = \$4,680$.

24. (b) $(12 \times 50) \times 1.15 = \$690$

25. (d) The furniture is sold through a dealer who would calculate price, so between the dealer and the designer (who specifies the furniture), the most accurate pricing will be calculated.

26. (b) Calculate the exact quantity needed for the most accurate estimates

Construction Drawings

27. (c) Locations of walls will be shown most completely on plan views; floor plan views will show partial-height walls, and ceiling plans will show full-height walls.

28. (d) Drafting conventions

29. (b) conventional illustration of concrete

30. (d) Product shown in solid wood but not enough info is given to presume answer b or c

Construction Specifications

31. (c) Loads are defined in anchorage devices, which is the performance descriptor asked about. Other options are material specifications.

32. (c) Any alternatives proposed by the contractor must be approved by the client or designer (depending on the contract) before substituting for the written specs.

33. (b) A proprietary spec identifies the exact product; other answer choices leave room for error or interpretation.

34. (d) Your verbal communication during the walk-through supplements your clear written instructions; N, S, E, W will not be clear enough for an irregularly shaped office. The best way to communicate this is with clear finish plans.

Section II: Contract Development and Administration

Contract Documents

35. (d) These are all contract documents and part of a legal contract.

36. (c) By the implementation phase, the designer has already specified furnishings and finishes, and the general contractor is responsible for coordination of trades; therefore, the only thing to do at this stage is answer c.

37. (d) The finish plan pertains to finishes, and the finish plan instructs the painter and paperhanger. Other trades refer to the finish plan in the normal course of their work but not the other three listed.

38. (a) Plan sets are arranged in a hierarchy with broad info followed by specific info. The overall identification and organization of the set is clarified; then plans precede details throughout the set.

39. (b) Commonly understood to mean b, unless identified as meaning something different

Furniture Fixtures and Equipment

40. (b) The wool/nylon blend will be the most durable, flame and stain resistant.

41. (d) Some of the tests listed are actually measures of sound (NRC and SRC) and pressure (PSI), which the student should recognize. Abrasion resistance and resistance to fading will be important in this space.

42. (a) Rayon will have the least resistance to fading.

43. (b) Classification A defines flammability.

Interior Construction

44. (c) This is a symbol for a metal stud, and it has only one layer of wallboard indicated.

45. (a) It is a construction that students should have encountered as meeting a 1-hour requirement.

46. (c) Interior designers are not qualified to make a judgment in cases of load-bearing, and other experts must be responsible for that. Plans may not reflect actual conditions so the safest thing to do is have the site inspected by a qualified professional.

47. (d) The danger of a person mistaking option d for an opening are reduced sufficiently for most codes to allow regular glass in this instance.

Finishes

48. (b) Peelable leaves a nice substrate for future paper installations, and the client will not have to have the paper steamed off the wall.

49. (c) The flat yet slip-resistant surface of the flamed granite will allow for easier maintenance than travertine or river rock.

50. (b) The most even installation will be the thickset. Random slate must have wide grout joints, eliminating unsanded grout; cork is not rigid enough for a material with no give, and dry-fit refers to a step during installation and not to an installation method.

51. (b) Options a and c will make the surfaces different from each other at the outset, and closed pore with filler will not really make a difference. However, option b brings consistency to the installation and protects it from changing differently over time due to light because it has UV protection.

Lighting

52. (c) Because color comparisons are so important, the ability of the lighting to render color accurately is the most crucial characteristic here.

53. (a) Sparkle is the most important contribution to crystal displays.

54. (c) Indirect ambient light will create less glare on computer screens, and being able to adjust light angles from a task light on the desk will avoid glare and control light levels for paper tasks.

55. (d) Electrical contractors install equipment according to plans by electrical engineers. Interior designers specify type and location of equipment, but the design of the entire system would be the responsibility of the electrical engineer on a large commercial job.

56. (c) Choice c maximizes contrast between risers and treads so the changing surfaces are easy to distinguish and the stairs will be safer.

Mechanical and Electrical Systems

57. (c) Matter of fact

58. (b) It is understood to be an exit light unless the legend states otherwise.

59. (a) Access floors are designed to run electrical and communication conduits, so they would not be the prohibited elements. Plumbing pipe is part of the building and must be installed per code, so water pipes would be prohibited.

60. (b) The danger is flame being drawn along air passage routes, so the solution is a fire damper that screens this passage of flame but allows air to move (unlike obstructions and insulation). Combustion in the plenum is secondary to flames being drawn through it.

Acoustics

61. (d) The most precise answer is d—it could be argued that it is accomplished by means such as those posed in option b, but it is not strictly a sound baffle.

62. (c) You want to deliver sound clearly, and oblique angles will break up the sound.

63. (a) It covers existing sound (of conversations) and can be monotonous, as it imitates the hum of equipment. It is usually employed to limit speech intelligibility from one space to another.

Communication Methods

64. (d) Matter of fact

65. (a) They illustrate a view as we are used to seeing it. They aren't the best options for portraying organization of space (plan view) or scale (elevation or isometric), and only one view is available in the drawing.

66. (d) Plan views are "bird's-eye" views.

67. (c) The drafting convention most typically employed uses line weight to visually strengthen items that stand in front of other items so they visually pop away from their backgrounds or to call attention to important elements of the drawing.

68. (a) Relative scale may be available in the plan view, but proportions are better shown in to-scale elevations, so a is the least true.

Building Codes

69. (b) Students should be able to distinguish between service and selling classifications for occupancy; this building is masonry (brick) and heavy timber construction and, anything over four stories is considered a high-rise.

70. (c) Exit enclosures are required to protect people exiting in the case of a fire in the building, so flame-spread ratings are more stringent in these areas regardless of the other classifications by which the building is defined.

Exiting

71. (d) Kitchens are considered to be hazardous areas and may not be used as part of an exit route.

72. (a) Required width cannot be reduced by door swings so it would be plus door swings; they must be accessible, and they can be used for normal use circulation too. They must comply with fire ratings assigned.

73. (b) Matter of fact

74. (a) This information is essential to looking up the distance limitations in code books.

75. (a) The number of people moving through the corridor has a direct impact on the required width.

Barrier Free

76. (d) Defined by ADA (Americans with Disabilities Act)

77. (b) Defined by ADA

78. (d) Option d will best protect the widest range of people.

79. (b) Options a, c, and d include dimensions above and below the most comfortable range.

Owner-Designer Agreements

80. (a) Options b, c, and d are all part of the cost of doing the work contracted for. Copying expense is not part of the design work and is usually reimbursable.

81. (c) The contractor building the niche has no reason to refer to the furnishings page; the complete info for constructing the niche is presumed to be on the partition plan. The error is the designer's, even if the partition drawings could be interpreted in more than one way.

82. (d) If you are efficient and bring the job in under the hourly estimate, you are penalized by lower fees. If you exceed the initial estimate, you work for free after you reach the estimate.

83. (b) Options a and d are requests for funds to be released; the bill of lading documents transport. It is the PO that accompanies the release of funds for a furniture purchase.

84. (b) Options c and d are illegal; the most direct way to solve the problem is to use the services of a structural engineer (architects often hire them as well as designers). Because there is little architectural planning required, an architect is more service than is needed.

Professional Practice

85. (c) Errors and omissions insurance is carried only by design professionals but the others would be a matter of contract dependant on the specific circumstances of the job.

86. (a) Marketing and PR do not supply goods and services needed to do business.

87. (a) More pointed efforts such as the brochure that you distribute where it is logical are better than expensive ads and scattershot mailings. Stationery is not a marketing plan.

88. (d) They are not the easiest to set up (sole proprietorship is).

Project Coordination

89. (a) The door was ordered from the manufacturer by the general contractor, and the opening was framed under the general contractor's contract.

90. (d) The POE evaluates the success of the current project.

91. (b) Options a, c, and d are implicit in the furniture contract as the responsibility of the furniture contractor, but option b can only be provided by the client.

92. (d) Option d is the responsibility of the design staff, not management.

93. (a) Confirming that the work is in compliance with specs is the primary responsibility of the designer. Just checking on the work (option b) is too passive. How the work is completed is not the domain of the designer—the outcome of the work is.

94. (c) All except option c are reasons to withhold approval payment if the work is "substantially complete."

Design Scenarios

DESIGN SCENARIO 1

Weaver's Studio, Full Version

WEAVER'S STUDIO

Full Version (145 points total)

Suggested Scoring Part One

These requirements *must* be met for 5 points each:

___ Living functions are not intermingled with studio functions.

___ Paths of travel from studio function do not have visual contact with living functions.

___ Safe egress is available to both functional spaces.

___ Plumbing circle is indicated by a dotted line.

(20 points)

The following *must* be met for 2 points each:

___ Egress is not blocked, locked, or used for storage.

___ Paths of egress are barrier free and are a minimum of 44 inches wide.

___ The shop, studio, and shop restroom are barrier free.

___ The weaver can exit the residence without going through the shop.

___ Doors along paths of exit travel are 36 inches wide and do not impinge upon clear 44-inch-wide path.

___ Open storage does not impinge on 44-inch-wide clear paths of exit travel.

___ Doors that are not along an exit path of travel are at least 30 inches clear open width.

___ Accessible doors have 18 inches clear wall space on the pull side of the latch edge and 12 inches on the push side of the latch edge.

___ Door swings do not encroach on turning circles.

___ Habitable spaces have natural light and ventilation.

___ The office and stock storage room are convenient to the shop but screened from customers.

___ The living area has direct access to the outdoors and to the shop.

___ Plumbing circle or 36-foot-diameter contains all plumbing fixtures.

___ The weaver can see the shop from their personal loom.

___ The point of sale station is centrally located and monitors the door.

___ 120 SF allocated for the office; office is screened from view of customers and has a 3 foot × 3 foot closet for phone equipment and circuit breaker.

___ 50 SF allocated for storage, screened from view of customers.

___ Studio location or orientation presents or implies a boundary to keep customers who are not students from wandering in.

___ Configuration screens the apartment from shop when the door between them is opened.

___ Bathroom is accessible to guests without requiring that they walk through the bedroom.

___ Solution is correctly portrayed entirely on sheet P1-2.

___ Adjacency matrix is complete and correct

(44 points)

The following *should* be shown on the matrix and the plan for 2 points each:

___ Direct adjacency Shop to Studio

___ Direct adjacency Weavers work area to Apartment

___ Direct adjacency Kitchen to Dining

___ Direct adjacency Bedroom to Bathroom

___ Convenient adjacency Shop to Office

___ Convenient adjacency Storage to Restroom

___ Convenient adjacency Living space to Bathroom

___ Material schedule
Retail shop floor F-2 walls W-4
Studio floor F-4 walls W-2
Weavers work area floor F-4 walls W-2
Restroom floor F-2 walls W-3

(16 points)

The following *should* be met for ¹/₂ point each:

Weaver Area

____ Loom 108 inches × 48 inches with bench

____ 21 LF of 10-inch-deep shelving

____ 30-inch-wide sink with 4 feet of counter to the right

Retail Shop

____ 20 (aggregate) LF of 20-inch-deep shelving

____ Three display tables 30 inches × 72 inches

____ Three stack of rugs 4 feet × 6 feet, 8 feet × 10 feet, and 6 feet × 9 feet with equal clear floor space immediately adjacent

____ Point of sale station minimum 2 feet × 5 feet

____ Lounge seating for 3 to 5 arranged for conversation

____ Snack buffet 18 SF of surface with access to storage below

____ Accessible restroom with storage cabinet and grab bars

Studio

____ Four looms 3 feet × 2 feet each with a chair

____ 30-inches × 2 wide sink with 4 feet of countertop to the right

____ 25 LF of shelving 18 inches deep

Living Area

____ Lounge seating for four with set-down surface reachable from each seat

____ Shelving unit holds TV 30 inches wide × 24 inches deep × 24 inches tall; stereo 18 inches wide × 17 inches deep × 15 inches tall and 40 LF bookcases (likely 7 feet wide unit if consolidated)

____ Convenient to entrance and guest coats

Dining Area

____ Table seating for 6

Kitchen

____ 15 LF of base and 10 LF of uppers

____ Refrigerator 30 inches × 28 inches × 72 inches tall

____ Dishwasher 2 feet × 2 feet

____ Microwave 21 inches wide × 18 inches deep

Bedroom

____ Double bed with minimum 2 feet clearance on each side

____ Nightstands 24 inches wide × 20 inches deep with clear space to access drawers below

____ Dresser 6 feet wide × 20 inches deep

____ Closet 5 feet wide showing three short hanging differentiated from 2 feet wide for double

Bathroom

____ Shower is indicated at end wall of tub

____ No item of furniture taller than 3 feet should be placed in front of windows with 3-foot-high sill

____ All required items are illustrated or labeled to differentiate from other item types

(14 points)

Suggested Scoring Part Two

These requirements *must* be met for 2 points each:

____ Plans are completed using only the selections and symbols given

____ Outlets are noted at 18 inches AFF except for the sales desk outlets and devices

____ Exit signage is located at both entrances and at the opening between the sitting area and the restrooms hallway

____ Outlets are wall outlets wherever practical

(8 points)

Desk Elevations

These requirements *must* be met for 2 points each:

____ The desk is accurately sketched or drafted to scale as required by elevation markers

____ The staff side indicates (with symbols or notes as appropriate) compartments for folded bags 6¹/₄ inches × 9¹/₄ inches, 8¹/₂ inches × 11 inches, 12 inches × 12 inches, and tissue paper 15 inches × 20 inches

____ The staff side indicates a phone jack and duplex outlet located in the vertical support for the tall transaction surface (30 inches to 40 inches AFF is a good range) and a data/power/phone 24 inches AFF behind closed doors and located below the space indicated for the cash register

___ Staff side has two trash containers conveniently located; each is 14 inches × 18 inches × 21 inches

___ Drawer space 24 inches wide (aggregate) and 6 inches tall

___ Locked cabinet 18 inches wide × 42 inches tall

___ Remaining space is presented as closed storage

___ Materials are noted

___ Sufficient dimensions to comprehend design, locations for services, and storage and size of storage spaces

(18 points)

Electrical Plan

The following *should* be met for 1 point each:

Sales Desk

___ Sales desk indicates the following equipment at the noted heights: phone/data/ power at 30 inches AFF, duplex outlet and phone at 30 inches to 40 inches AFF

___ Duplex outlet under transaction surface

___ Phone line 24 inches AFF

Diorama

___ Duplex floor outlet at this location

Consultant Office

___ Duplex in wall next to desk

___ Phone jack in wall next to desk

___ Voice/data/power in wall next to desk

Equipment Closet

___ Voice/data/power in wall in closet

___ Quad in wall in closet

Shop

___ Wall duplex in side of table

___ Two duplex wall outlets in shelving

___ Washroom

___ Duplex GFI in wall near sink

(13 points)

Lighting

These requirements *must* be met for 1 point each:

___ Fluorescent lighting used for ambient light to meet energy-conservation requirement

___ Minimum one fixture in each sales office

___ Minimum one light fixture in electrical closet and in each bathroom

___ Minimum five light fixtures in open area

___ Minimum one light fixture in hallway near electrical closet

___ Exit signage visible from all locations in open areas and hallways

___ Lighting controls properly communicated with circuitry

Additional point awarded for good decisions such as:

___ Flexible lighting for display surfaces (diorama, shelving, and tabletop)

___ Task light on sales desk and consultant desks

___ Fan/light in restrooms

___ Emergency lighting is part of scheme

___ Each incandescent lamp and foot of incandescent strip used multiplied by 2, plus each fluorescent and exit light multiplied by 1, should not add up to more than 50

(12 points)

TIMED DESIGN EXERCISE

Instructions to Students

1. Read all of these instructions before beginning the exercise.
2. Review the project and code requirements as well as the site plan P1-1.
3. Review the matrix, material options, and material schedules P1-1.
4. Review the interior elevation showing the window fenestration from the interior P1-1.
5. Review the floor plan P1-2.
6. Read the entire project description and carefully review the requirements in each area.
7. Complete the adjacency matrix P1-1.
8. Show your proposed layout on the sheet given to solve the problem defined (following).
9. Select finish materials for the floors and walls and indicate the best choice by circling it on the schedule P1-1.
10. Write your control number in the lower right of every sheet—even the ones that you don't write on.

Code Requirements

- All exterior doors are available for egress as they swing out and have a minimum clear opening of 3'.
- Egress paths of travel may not pass through areas that may be blocked, locked, or used for storage.
- Barrier free requires a 5' turning circle (show as a dotted line) at every change in direction. Paths of travel not required for egress are not bound by this restriction.
- Egress must be provided from the residence without requiring the weaver to pass through the shop to exit.
- Maintain a minimum width of 44" along accessible routes.
- Doors and storage units that open toward a path of travel may not limit the clear passage width when open.
- Doors to be a minimum of 3' clear width in all accessible spaces and a minimum 30" clear width otherwise.
- Doors in accessible areas must be flanked by clear wall space 18" on the pull side and 12" wide on the push side along the latching side.
- Sinks in barrier-free areas must have clear knee space below and may not encroach on the turning circle.
- Door swings may not encroach on turning circles.
- Habitable spaces in the living space/apartment must have an operable window.
- Floors in areas with sinks must be slip resistant.
- Surfaces in bathrooms and washrooms must be moisture resistant.

Design Requirements

All items, adjacencies, and attributes mentioned in this document are required in your passing solution. Use a freehand sketch or drafting to represent items in accurate scale. Draw your solution on drawing sheets provided using ink or felt tip (it will be assumed that all pencil is preliminary to your final solution and not intended as part of your final solution). You need only erase pencil marks that will interfere with comprehension of your solution.

Complete the partition and furniture plan on P1-1, showing typical required details (door swings, backs on chairs, pillows on bed, etc.) to the extent necessary to distinguish one type of item from another. Label all spaces listed in the project description. Include the lineal feet or cubic feet of storage required with the label for such items where the specific requirement is noted on the project requirements list.

Project Description

In a rural vacation destination, a varied group of artisans creates and sells their work within an enclave of small separate buildings. A weaver lives, works, and teaches weaving at the project location. The living area is to be located to have discreet access from the shop and is also to have direct access to the outside. Classes are held in the shop after the close of business. The shop, studio for classes, and the shop restroom are to be handicapped accessible. An office for managing business and a storage room for extra stock is to be conveniently accessed from the shop but screened from customers.

Plumbing locations should all be within a 36' diameter circle (circle location to be determined by you and indicated on the plan with a dotted line). The building shell with windows and doors as indicated cannot be changed; the exterior of the building cannot be changed. Access flooring is used throughout EXCEPT in the apartment bathroom and kitchen and in the shop washroom. Except for the windows in the two projecting corners, the windows are 3' from finished floor to bottom of the apron. The projecting windows in the NW and SE are 18" from floor to sill.

Requirements for each functional area follow. Address the items to be represented as well as adjacencies and privacy considerations. Functions may be combined as long as all requirements are met.

Shop Area

Weaver's Work Area
1. Loom 108" wide and 48" deep with a seat for the weaver
2. 21 lineal feet of shelving that is 10" deep and provides 10" of height per shelf for cones and baskets of yarn
3. Sink 30" wide × 18" deep from front to back with 4' of counter surface to the right

The weaver works at the loom when there are no customers in the shop, so it must be possible to visually monitor the shop from the loom, but customers must not have access to this area. This area need not be handicapped accessible.

Retail Shop
1. Full-height display shelving 20" deep and a total/aggregate width of 20' (need not be contiguous).
2. Three separate tabletop displays 30" × 72" with storage below. Tables are on locking casters.
3. Clear floor space for stacks of rugs organized in piles by size. Each stack to have a clear floor space of the same size as the rug, immediately adjacent to the rug for comparing two rugs of the same size to each other. Show the rug location with a solid line and the clear area with a dotted line. Rug sizes are 4' × 6', 8' × 10', 6' × 9'.
4. Point-of-sale station/cash-wrap 2'-6" deep × 5' wide minimum must be centrally located and salesperson must be able to monitor the doors.
5. Lounge seating for 3 to 5 persons arranged for conversation.
6. Surface for a snack buffet that provides 18 square feet of surface has storage below for glasses, mugs, and plates.
7. Accessible restroom with toilet, sink, storage cabinet 10" deep × 2' wide, which should also be accessible. Label grab bars.

This area is used for promotional events that have a social atmosphere, and food and drinks are served at these functions. The weaver also entertains friends who stop by after hours. This area must be accessible.

Office
1. Allocate room 120 square feet
2. Closet within room for phone and computer equipment full height 3' × 3'

Storage
1. Allocate 80 square feet for woven goods for resale

Studio Classroom
1. Four looms 3' wide × 2' deep from front to back, each with a chair
2. Sink 30" wide × 18" deep with 4' of clear counter space to the right
3. 45 lineal feet of 18" deep shelving, each shelf having 12" of height

This area may be open to the shop but must be a distinctly separate area so customers do not disturb student work on the looms. This area must be accessible.

Living Space for Weaver

Guest coats must be stored immediately adjacent to the door from the outside. The configuration of the entrance area, directly from the shop, should provide visual privacy when the door is opened. The living space/apartment need not be accessible.

Living Space/Apartment

Sitting Room
1. Lounge seating for four
2. Set-down surface at each seat
3. Shelving unit containing TV 30" wide × 24" deep × 28" tall, stacked stereo equipment requires 18" wide × 17" deep × 15" tall space when stacked; 40 lineal feet of book shelving

Dining
1. Table and chairs for 6 people

Kitchen
1. 15 lineal feet clear counter space over base cabinets and appliances
2. 10 lineal feet of upper cabinets
3. Full-height refrigerator 30" wide × 28" deep
4. Undercounter dishwasher 24" × 24"
5. Microwave 21" wide × 18" deep × 15" tall
6. Sink 24" wide × 18" deep from front to back
7. Range 24" wide × 30" deep

Sleep Space
1. Double bed 54" wide × 75" long
2. Pair of nightstands 24" wide × 20" deep × 26" tall, with drawer storage
3. Dresser 6' wide × 20" deep from front to back × 30" tall
4. Closet with 3' of long hanging and 4' of short/double hanging

Bathroom
1. Vanity cabinet 30" wide × 22" deep containing sink
2. Toilet
3. Tub 2'-5" wide × 5'-0" long with shower. Indicate location of fittings (shower head and faucet)
4. Linen closet 24" wide × 24" deep full height

The toilet and sink must be accessible to guests without requiring that they pass through the sleep space. The bathroom must be immediately adjacent to the sleep space.

Timed Design Exercise

Part 1 of 2

Part One of Design Exercise
Weaver's Studio, Full Version

Sheet: C-1

Scale: None

Student Control Number

Weaver's Studio, Full Version

Site Plan
Elevation
Matrix
Schedule

Sheet

P1-1

Scale   As Noted

Control Number

Adjacency Matrix
Use only these symbols; do not make up your own symbols.

● Direct Adjacency
○ Convenient Adjacency
☐ Visual Connection
X Remote

	Retail Shop	Studio	Work Area	Restroom	Office	Storage	LR/Ent.	Kitchen	Dining	Sleeping	Bath
Retail Shop											
Studio											
Work Area											
Restroom											
Office											
Storage											
LR/Ent.											
Kitchen											
Dining											
Sleeping											
Bath											

F	Floor
F1	45 oz level loop nylon carpet tiles loose lay
F2	Stained concrete sealed 3 coats matte nonslip urethane
F3	Ungauged slate with heavy cleft face acrylic high-gloss sealer
F4	Recycled rubber tiles size coordinated with access floor
F5	Linoleum sheet goods
W	Walls
W1	Linen wall covering not fire-rated
W2	Semigloss, low VOC paint
W3	Ceramic tile
W4	Textured commercial vinyl wall covering

Circle the most appropriate choice from those listed to the right by referencing the table above for material descriptions.

Area	Floor			Walls		
Retail Shop	F1	F2	F5	W1	W3	W4
Studio	F5	F4	F1	W1	W2	W3
Work Area	F5	F4	F4	W1	W2	W3
Restroom	F1	F2	F4	W1	W3	W4

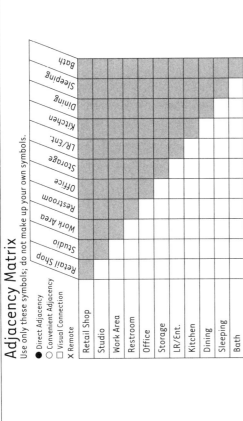

N ←

A Site Plan

Roof Structure
Finished Ceiling
Window – fixed pane over operable in-swinging hopper
Access Flooring
connector

B Interior Elevation
Scale 1/8" = 1'-0"

Weaver's Studio, Full Version   **Timed Design Exercises**   Part 1 of 2   **CD**

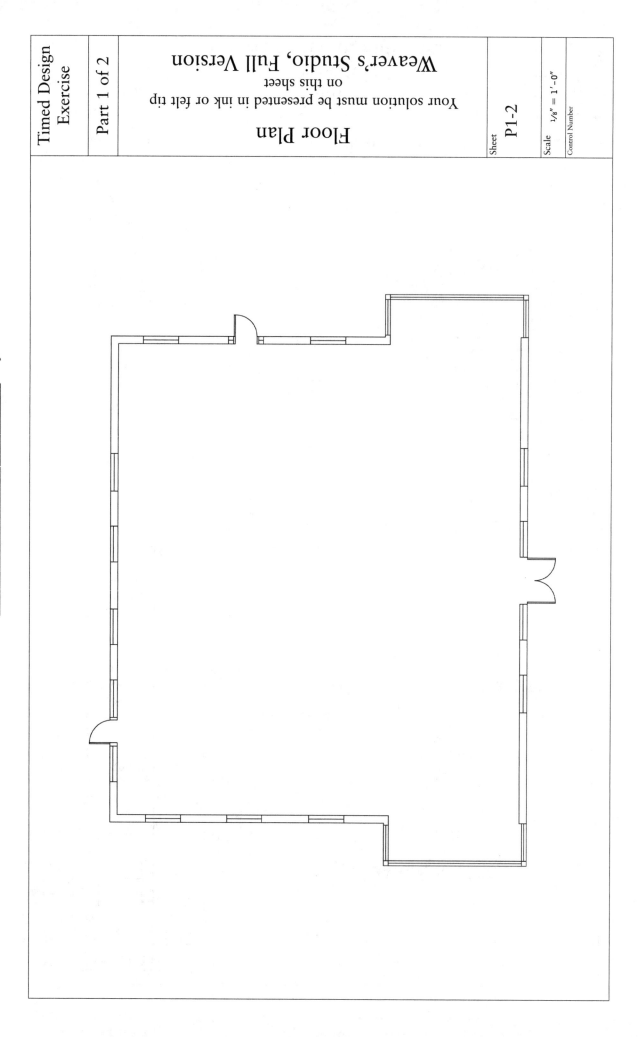

Timed Design Exercise		Floor Plan		
Part 1 of 2		Weaver's Studio, Full Version on this sheet Your solution must be presented in ink or felt tip		
		Sheet **P1-2**	Scale 1/8" = 1'-0"	Control Number

TIMED DESIGN EXERCISE

Instructions to Students

1. Read all of these instructions before beginning the exercise.
2. Review the project and code requirements and additional scope of services.
3. Review the floor plan P2-1; notice the layout for your lighting and electrical planning and also the elevation symbols indicating the two elevations for the sales desk, which are to be drawn on sheet P2-1 at $1/4'' = 1'0''$ (requirements follow).
4. Review all of the symbols and electrical requirements on sheet P2-2.
5. Locate the electrical and communication devices required on the electrical/data/phone plan, sheet P2-2.
6. Create a reflected ceiling plan on sheet P2-3 showing all lighting locations.
7. Draw required circuitry and switching locations for a functional design.
8. Write your control number where indicated in the lower right corner of every sheet—even the ones that you don't write on.
9. Select the best choice from the equipment listed in the legends and use only that equipment and those symbols. Do not add equipment or make up your own symbols.

Code Requirements

All electrical outlets must be located 18'' AFF unless noted otherwise.
- Exit signage must be visible upon exiting all enclosed spaces and positioned to direct people safely out of the building without confusion as to the exit locations.
- Where practical, wall outlets and ports are preferred over floor-mounted outlets and ports.
- Electricity, voice, and data devices required of the sales desk are to be brought up into and permanently affixed within the built-in sales desk.
- Electricity, voice, and data devices for sales offices will not be brought up into the portable desks and must be configured so no cords span open space where a person might walk.

Additional Scope of Services

The sales center for the artisans country enclave serves a few functions. It houses offices for sales associates who reserve rental units for families who vacation on the property and a small souvenir shop. It functions as a warming house in the winter and makes restrooms available for people enjoying the grounds; there is also a pond adjacent to the building.

Design Requirements

All items, adjacencies, and attributes mentioned in this document are required in your solution. Use a freehand sketch or drafting to represent items in accurate scale. Draw your solution on drawing sheets provided using ink or felt tip (it will be assumed that all pencil is preliminary to your final solution and not intended as part of your final solution).

Project Description

Sales Desk
1. The design of the sales desk is to be congruent with nature and art themes.
2. A computerized cash register sits on the sales counter 30'' AFF and is networked to a hard drive in the equipment closet. The device that connects and powers the register is to be located 24'' AFF in a closed-door storage unit within the sales desk, below the register.
3. A phone is also located on the desk, connected and powered by a device located in the vertical support for the transaction top.
4. Three kinds/sizes of bags and one size of tissue paper are to be organized in individual compartments. Folded bag sizes are 6.25'' × 9.25'', 8.5'' × 11'', and 12'' × 12''. Tissue paper is 15'' × 20''.
5. Two trash containers (one for paper, one for trash) are each 14'' × 18'' × 21'' tall.
6. Drawer space for supplies to be aggregately (need not be a single drawer) 24'' wide with a 6'' tall drawer face (for a 5'' tall drawer box) and 18'' deep with full-extension glides.
7. One locked cabinet for staff personal belongings to be minimally 18'' wide × 24'' tall, full cabinet depth.
8. Additional closed storage with one adjustable shelf per unit as possible.
9. Label all finishes/surface materials for the desk; note incremental and overall dimensions.
10. Indicate with hidden lines and a note the barrier-free transaction surface at 30'' high.
11. Draw and note a second transaction surface at 45'' high.
12. A convenience outlet is to be located in the vertical support for the 45'' high transaction surface.

Electrical Plan
1. Review the requirements on sheet P2-2 and provide for all required devices.
2. The tabletop displays for sales and diorama of the grounds are 30'' above finished floor.

Lighting/Reflected Ceiling Plan
1. Energy conservation to be balanced with effective lighting techniques in display and sales area.
2. Solution to be safe and conform with codes.

Part Two of Design Exercise
Weaver's Studio, Full Version

Sheet

C-2

Scale   None

Student Control Number

Use the space below to draw (to scale) your design for the sales desk showing all equipment devices, dimensions, and material descriptions.

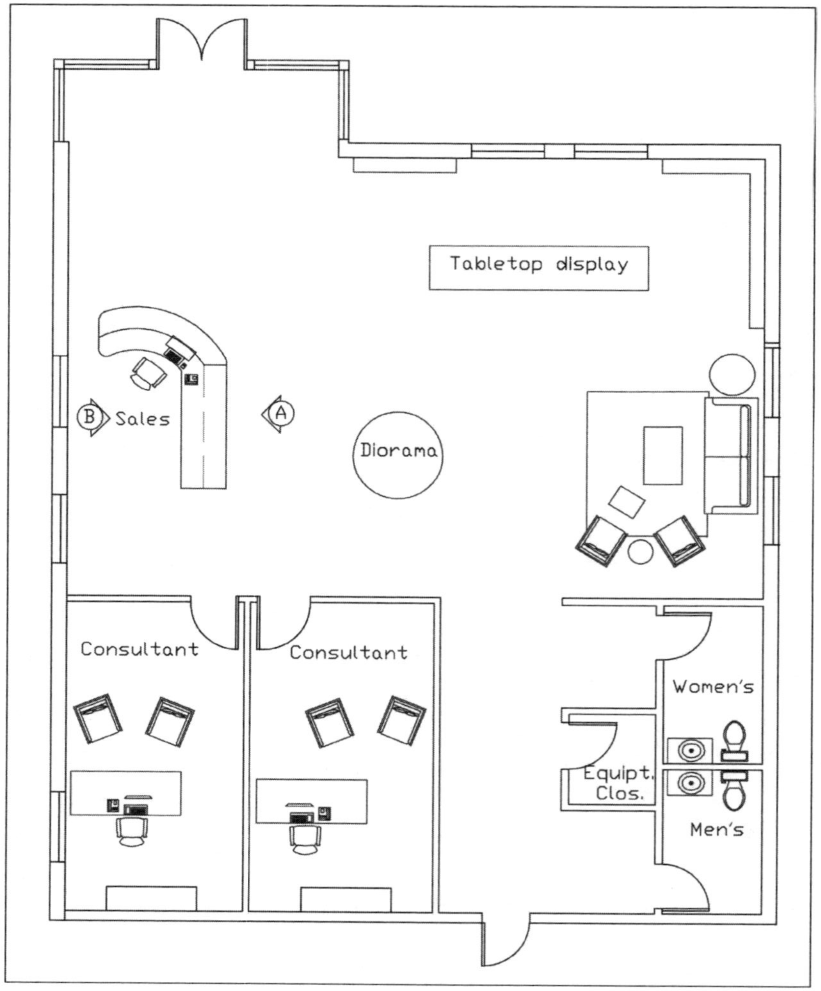
Tabletop display
Sales
B
A
Diorama
Consultant
Consultant
Women's
Men's
Equipt. Clos.

Timed Design Exercise

Part 2 of 2

Floor Plan
Weaver's Studio, Full Version

Sheet P2-1

Scale 1/8″ = 1′-0″

Control Number

(A) Elevation of Customer Side of Sales Desk
Scale: 1/4″ = 1′-0″

(B) Elevation of Staff Side of Sales Desk
Scale: 1/4″ = 1′-0″

Timed Design Exercise

Part 2 of 2

Electrical/Data/Phone Plan
Weaver's Studio, Full Version

Sheet

P2-2

Scale   1/8" = 1'-0"

Control Number

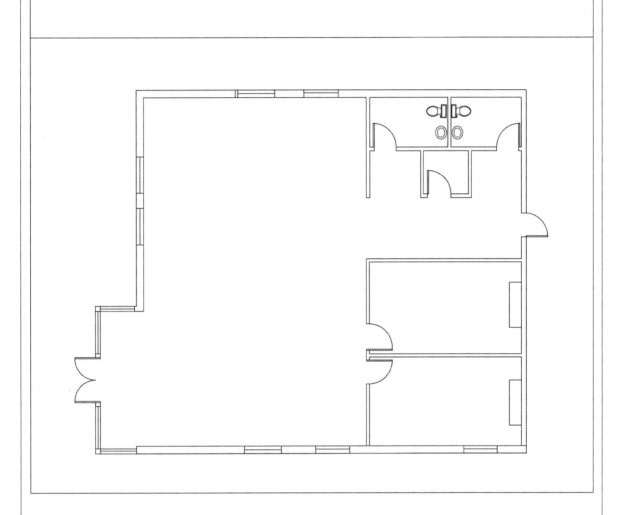

Electrical Legend

Symbol	Description
⊕	Duplex outlet
⊕GFI	Ground Fault Interrupt duplex outlet
⊕	Quadruplex outlet
⊕	220-volt outlet
▽	Cat 3 phone port
▼	Cat 5 data port
▽	Voice and data port
▼	Voice/data/power
⊡	Floor duplex outlet
▽	Floor phone port
▼	Floor data port

Use only these symbols to communicate your design. Do not make up your own symbols.

Equipment List   Note all heights that deviate from typical 18" AFF

Qty	Location and requirements
1	Sales desk: phone/data/power in desktop
1	Sales desk: one duplex outlet under transaction counter
1	Sales desk: one phone line 24" AFF for computer
1	Diorama: duplex in floor under pedestal
1	Consultant desk: duplex each office
1	Consultant desk: phone/data/power each office
1	Consultant desk: phone each office
2	Equipt closet: phone/data/power closet
2	Equipment closet: quadruplex outlet closet
1	Tabletop display: one duplex each mounted in side
2	Display shelving wall: duplex outlets 45" AFF
1	Washroom one GFI outlet at sink in each restroom

Refer to this list as you prepare your electrical/data/power plan; select and show only these items on that plan.

Weaver's Studio, Full Version | Timed Design Exercises | Part 2 of 2 (CD)

Lighting Legend

Wall	Ceiling	
	ⓡ	Recessed incandescent
⊢Ⓛⱽ	ⓡ LV	Recessed incandescent low voltage
⊢Ⓕ	ⓡ CFL	Recessed compact fluorescent
	⬛	Recessed fluorescent troffer
– – –	– – –	Hidden light fixture fluorescent T5 or xenon strip light
	⊗	Portable task or table lamp
	▷	Track lighting—broad side of triangle indicates beam side
⊢Ⓡ E	ⓡ E	Security lighting with backup battery power (always on)
⊗	⊗	Exit sign (dark portion indicates location of lettering)
	FL	Exhaust fan/light
⨉		Light switch
⨉₃		3-pole switch
⨉ᴅ		Dimmer switch

Refer to this list as you prepare your Lighting Plan; show only these items on your plan; use only these fixtures to solve the problem and only these symbols—do not make up your own symbols.

Timed Design Exercise

Part 2 of 2

Reflected Ceiling Plan
Weaver's Studio, Full Version

Sheet	**P2-3**
Scale	1/8" = 1'-0"
Control Number	

DESIGN SCENARIO 1
Weaver's Studio, Lite Version

WEAVER'S STUDIO

Lite Version (121 points total)

Suggested Scoring Part One

The following *must* be met for 5 points each:

___ Living functions are not intermingled with studio functions.

___ Paths of travel from studio function do not have visual contact with living functions other than entry and powder room functions.

___ Safe egress is available to both functional spaces.

___ Plumbing circle is indicated on plan with dotted line.

___ Solution does not require change to building shell to be successful.

(25 points)

The following *must* be met for 2 points each (code requirements listed on C-1 and matrix on P1-1 plus code requirements that should be known):

___ Egress is not blocked, locked, or used for storage.

___ Paths of egress are barrier free and are a minimum of 44 inches wide.

___ The entrance, studio, and restroom are barrier free.

___ The weaver can exit residence more than one way.

___ Doors along paths of exit travel are 36 inches wide and do not impinge upon clear 44-inch-wide path.

___ Open storage does not impinge on 44-inch-wide clear paths of exit travel.

___ Doors that are not along an exit path of travel are at least 30 inches clear open width.

___ Accessible doors have 18 inches clear wall space on the pull side of the latch edge and 12 inches on the pull side of the hinge edge.

___ Grab bars are shown in barrier-free bathrooms.

___ Door swings do not encroach on turning circles.

___ Habitable spaces have natural light and ventilation.

___ Bedroom has reasonable fire-escape options.

___ Solution is correctly portrayed entirely on sheet P1-2.

___ Adjacency matrix is complete and correct.

(28 points)

The following should be shown on the matrix and the plan for 1 point each:

___ Direct adjacency BR to Bath

___ Direct adjacency Kitchen to Dining

___ Convenient adjacency Studio to Powder Room

___ Convenient adjacency Living Room to Powder Room

___ Residence to studio visually screened

___ Material schedule
Living/entertainment Floor F-1 walls W-4
Kitchen floor F-4 walls W-2
Studio floor F-4 walls W-2
Studio Restroom floor F-2 walls W-4

(6 points)

The following *should* be met for 1/2 point each:

Weaver's Studio Area

___ Loom 108 inches wide × 48 inches deep with seat

___ Visual connection between this area and student looms

___ Four looms 3 feet × 2 feet each with a chair

___ 21 LF shelving 10 inches deep

___ Sink 30 inches wide × 18 inches deep with 4 feet of counter to the right

___ Four drying racks 4 feet wide × 18 inches deep

Planning Area

___ Lounge seating for five arranged so seats face each other

___ Drafting board 3 feet × 2 feet with seat

___ Desk with two pedestals dotted in

___ Copy/print/fax stand 20 inches × 20 inches storage below accessible from one side

Restroom

___ Toilet

___ Sink

___ Grab bars labeled

Entrance to Residence from Outside

___ Guest coat storage indicated

___ Entrance from shop allows visual privacy for residence

Living/Entertainment Room

___ Lounge seating for four

___ Set-down surface at each seat

___ Shelving minimum 2½ feet wide × 2 feet deep

___ 40 LF of book shelving

Kitchen

___ 5 LF of base

___ 3 LF of uppers

___ Refrigerator 30 inches × 28 inches × 72 inches tall

___ Range 2 feet × 2 feet

___ Microwave 21 inches wide × 18 inches deep

___ Sink 36 inches × 18 inches

Sleep Space

___ Double bed 54 inches wide × 75 inches long

___ Pair of nightstands 24 inches wide × 20 inches deep

___ Dresser 6 feet wide × 20 inches deep

___ Closet 5 LF hanging minimum

Bathroom

___ Vanity 30 inches wide× 22 inches deep

___ Toilet

___ Tub 2 feet-5 inches × 5 feet

___ Linen closet 2 feet × 2 feet

___ Toilet and sink are accessible to guests without having to go through bedroom

(17 points)

Suggested Scoring Part Two

The following should be met for 2 points each:

___ Plans are completed using only the selections and symbols given

___ Outlets are noted at 18 inches AFF except for the sales desk outlets and devices

___ Exit signage positioned for visibility from all locations (except inside washroom)

___ Outlets are wall outlets wherever practical, including eight laptop outlet locations

___ No electrical cords span open space to serve equipment from wall outlets

(10 points)

Desk Elevations

The following should be met for 2 points each:

___ Cash register device located 24 inches AFF in a closed door storage, and cash drawer below the register

___ Four compartments for bags and tissue paper

___ Two trash containers 14 inches × 18 inches × 21 inches tall

___ Closed storage with one adjustable shelf per unit shown in unassigned areas

___ Labeled all finishes/surface materials congruent with nature and art themes

___ Noted incremental and overall dimensions. Hidden lines and notes indicate requirements unseen in required views

___ Barrier-free transaction surface. Second transaction surface at 45 inches high

(14 points)

Electrical Plan

The following should be met for 1 point each:

Service Counter

___ Voice/data/power in desktop

___ Phone 24 inches AFF

___ Voice/data/power in wall at each advisor desk

Shop Area

___ Floor duplex under diorama

___ Two outlets in shelving at 45 inches AFF

Advisors' Offices

___ Phone jack in wall at each advisor desk

___ Two quad outlets in wall in equipment closet

___ Two voice/data/power in wall in equipment closet

Washroom

___ GFI at sink

Lighting Plan

___ Fluorescent lights for ambient light

___ Incandescent used only for accent and display

___ Exit signage visible from all locations in shop (outside of restroom)

___ Minimum three light fixtures in shop

___ Minimum one light fixture in each restroom

___ Minimum one light fixture in hallway

___ Minimum one light fixture in electrical closet

___ Minimum one light fixture in advisors' offices

(17 points)

One point awarded for:

___ Fan/light in bathroom

___ Emergency lighting incorporated into scheme

___ Task lighting provided at advisor's desk

___ Each incandescent lamp and foot of incandescent strip used multiplied by 2, plus each fluorescent and exit light multiplied by 1, should not add up to more than 40

(4 points)

TIMED DESIGN EXERCISE

Instructions to Students

1. Read all of these instructions before beginning the exercise.
2. Review the project and code requirements as well as the site plan P1-1.
3. Review the matrix, material options, and material schedules.
4. Review the interior elevation showing the window fenestration from the interior P1-1.
5. Review the floor plan P1-2.
6. Read the entire project description and carefully review the requirements in each area.
7. Complete the adjacency matrix P1-1.
8. Show your proposed layout on the sheet given to solve the problem defined (following).
9. Select finish materials for the floors and walls and indicate the best choice by circling it on the schedule P1-1.
10. Write your control number in the lower right of every sheet—even the ones that you don't write on.

Code Requirements

- All exterior doors are available for egress as they swing out and have a minimum clear opening of 3'.
- Egress paths of travel may not pass through areas that may be blocked, locked, or used for storage.
- Barrier free requires a 5" turning circle (show as a dotted line) at every change in direction. Paths of travel not required for egress are not bound by this restriction.
- Egress must be provided from the residence without requiring the weaver to pass through the shop to exit.
- Maintain a minimum width of 44" along accessible routes.
- Doors and storage units that open toward a path of travel may not limit the clear passage width when open.
- Doors to be a minimum of 3' clear width in all accessible spaces and a minimum 30' clear width otherwise.
- Doors in accessible areas must be flanked by clear wall space 18" on the pull side and 12" wide on the push side along the latching side.
- Sinks in barrier-free areas must have clear knee space below and may not encroach on the turning circle more than 6".
- Door swings may not encroach on turning circles.
- Habitable spaces in the living space/apartment must have an operable window.
- Floors in areas with sinks must be slip resistant.
- Surfaces in bathrooms and washrooms must be moisture resistant.

Design Requirements

All items, adjacencies, and attributes mentioned in this document are required in your passing solution. Use a freehand sketch or drafting to represent items in accurate scale. Draw your solution on drawing sheets provided using ink or felt tip (it will be assumed that all pencil is preliminary to your final solution and not intended as part of your final solution). You need only erase pencil marks that will interfere with comprehension of your solution.

Complete the partition and furniture plan on P1-1 showing typical required details (door swings, backs on chairs, pillows on bed, etc.) to the extent necessary to distinguish one type of item from another. Label all spaces listed in the project description. Include the lineal feet or cubic feet of storage required with the label for such items where the specific requirement is noted on the project requirements list.

Project Description

The project is a rural art camp for gifted high school–level students who spend 2 months studying with an artist on a selected medium. A graduate art student who is a weaver lives, works, and teaches weaving at the project location. The living area is to be located to have discreet access from the studio and is also to have direct access to the outside. Classes are held in the studio. The studio and restroom in it are to be handicapped accessible.

Plumbing locations should all be within a 20' diameter circle (circle location to be determined by you and indicated on the plan with a dotted line). The exterior of the building cannot be changed; the location cannot be changed; the exterior of the building cannot be changed. Access flooring is used throughout EXCEPT in the apartment bathroom and kitchen and in the shop washroom. Except for the windows in the two projecting corners, the windows are 3' from finished floor to bottom of the apron. The projecting windows in the NW and SE are 18" from floor to sill.

Requirements for each functional area follow. Address the items to be represented as well as adjacencies and privacy considerations. Functions may be combined as long as all requirements are met.

Shop Area

Weaver's Studio Area

1. Loom 108" wide and 48" deep with a seat for the weaver. The weaver works at this loom while students are busy at their own looms, so it must be possible to visually monitor the students while seated at this loom.
2. Four looms 3' wide × 2' deep from front to back, each with a chair
3. 21 lineal feet of shelving that is 10" deep and provides 10" of height per shelf for cones and baskets of yarn
4. Sink 30" wide × 18" deep from front to back with 4' of counter surface to the right
5. Four drying racks 4' wide × 18" deep

Planning Area

1. Lounge seating for 5 persons arranged for conversation
2. One drafting board 36" wide × 24" deep with stool
3. Desk with double file pedestals and computer.
4. Combination copier, printer, and scanner on its own stand, which is 20" wide × 20" deep. Paper and supplies stored below.
5. This area may be combined with weaving studio as long as all requirements are met.

Restroom

1. Accessible restroom with toilet, sink, storage cabinet 10" deep × 2' wide. Label grab bars.

Living Space for Weaver

Living Space/Apartment

Sitting Room

1. Lounge seating for four with a set-down surface at each seat
2. Shelving unit containing TV 30" wide × 24" deep × 28" tall; stacked stereo equipment requires 18" wide × 17" deep × 15" tall space when stacked; 40 lineal feet of book shelving
3. Dining table and chairs for 4 people

Kitchen

1. 5 lineal feet clear counter space over base cabinets and appliances in addition to sink and range
2. 3 lineal feet of upper cabinets
3. Full-height refrigerator 30" wide × 28" deep
4. Range 24" × 24"
5. Microwave 21" wide × 18" deep × 15" tall
6. Sink with integral drain board 36" wide × 18" deep from front to back

Sleep Space

1. Double bed 54" wide × 75" long
2. Pair of nightstands 24" wide × 20" deep × 26" tall, with drawer storage
3. Dresser 6' wide × 20" deep from front to back × 30" tall
4. Closet with 3' of long hanging and 4' of short/double hanging

Bathroom

1. Vanity cabinet 30" wide × 22" deep containing sink
2. Toilet
3. Tub 2'-5" wide × 5'-0" long with shower. Indicate location of fittings (shower head and faucet)

The toilet and sink must be accessible to guests without requiring that they pass through the sleep space. The bathroom must be immediately adjacent to the sleep space.

Guest coats must be stored immediately adjacent to the door from the outside. The configuration of the entrance area, directly from the shop, should provide visual privacy for the living space when the door is opened. The living space/apartment need not be accessible.

Part One of Design Exercise
Weaver's Studio, Lite Version

Timed Design Exercise

Part 1 of 2

Sheet

C–1

Scale   None

Student Control Number

Weaver's Studio, Lite Version

Site Plan
Elevation
Matrix
Schedule

Sheet

P1-1

Scale   As Noted

Control Number

Adjacency Matrix
Use only these symbols; do not make up your own symbols.

● Direct Adjacency
○ Convenient Adjacency
X Remote

	Studio	Retail Area	Restroom	LR/Ent.	Kitchen	Sleeping	Bath
Studio							
Retail Area							
Restroom							
LR/Ent.							
Kitchen							
Sleeping							
Bath							

F	Floor
F1	45 oz level loop nylon carpet tiles loose lay
F2	Stained concrete sealed 3 coats matte nonslip urethane
F3	Ungauged slate with heavy cleft face acrylic high-gloss sealer
F4	Recycled rubber tiles size coordinated with access floor
F5	Linoleum sheet goods
W	Walls
W1	Linen wall covering not fire-rated
W2	Semi-gloss, low VOC paint
W3	Ceramic tile
W4	Textured commercial vinyl wall covering

Area	Floor			Walls		
Living/Ent	F1	F2	F5	W1	W3	W4
Kitchen	F1	F4	F5	W1	W2	W3
Studio	F3	F4	F5	W1	W2	W3
Studio WC	F1	F2	F4	W1	W2	W4

Circle the most appropriate choice from those listed to the right by referencing the table above for material descriptions.

N

(A) Site Plan

(B) Interior Elevation
Scale 1/8" = 1'-0"

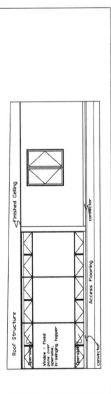

Roof Structure
Finished Ceiling
Access Flooring
Window – fixed pane over operable, in-swinging hopper
operable
operable
connector
connector

Timed Design Exercise		
Part 1 of 2		

Weaver's Studio, Lite Version

Your solution must be presented in ink or felt tip on this sheet

Floor Plan

Sheet	**P1-2**
Scale	1/8" = 1'-0"
Control Number	

TIMED DESIGN EXERCISE

Part Two of Design Exercise
Weaver's Studio, Lite Version

Sheet

C-2

Scale   None

Student Control Number

Instructions to Students

1. Read all of these instructions before beginning the exercise.
2. Review the project and code requirements and additional scope of services.
3. Review the floor plan P2-1; notice the layout for your lighting and electrical planning and also the elevation symbols indicating the two elevations for the sales desk, which are to be drawn on sheet P2-1 at 1/4" = 1'-0" (requirements follow).
4. Review all of the symbols and electrical requirements on sheet P2-2.
5. Locate the electrical and communication devices required on the electrical/data/phone plan, sheet P2-2.
6. Create a reflected ceiling plan on sheet P2-3 showing all lighting locations.
7. Draw required circuitry and switching locations for a functional design.
8. Write your control number where indicated in the lower right corner of every sheet—even the ones that you don't write on.
9. Select the best choice from the equipment listed in the legends and use only that equipment and those symbols. Do not add equipment or make up your own symbols.

Code Requirements

• All electrical outlets must be located 18" AFF unless noted otherwise.
• Exit signage must be visible upon exiting all enclosed spaces and positioned to direct people safely out of the building without confusion as to the exit locations.
• Where practical, wall outlets and ports are preferred over floor-mounted outlets and ports.
• Electricity, voice, and data devices required of the sales desk are to be brought up into and permanently affixed within the built-in sales desk.
• Electricity, voice, and data devices for sales offices will not be brought up into the portable desks and must be configured so no cords span open space where a person might walk.

Additional Scope of Services

The camp office center serves a few functions. It houses offices for advisors and organizers, and houses a small shop with toiletries and other commonly needed supplies. Restrooms are available for people enjoying the grounds, and there is a pond adjacent to the building.

Design Requirements

All items, adjacencies, and attributes mentioned in this document are required in your solution. Use a freehand sketch or drafting to represent items in accurate scale. Draw your solution on drawing sheets provided using ink or felt tip (it will be assumed that all pencil is preliminary to your final solution and not intended as part of your final solution).

Sales Counter

1. The design of the sales desk is to be congruent with nature and art themes.
2. A computerized cash register sits on the sales counter 36" AFF and is networked to a hard drive in the equipment closet. The device that connects and powers the register is to be located 24" AFF in a closed-door storage unit within the sales desk, below the register.
3. A phone is also located on the desk, connected and powered by a device located in the vertical support for the transaction top.
4. Three kinds/sizes of bags and one size of tissue paper are to be organized in individual compartments. Folded bag sizes are 6.25" × 9.25", 8.5" × 11", and 12" × 12". Tissue paper is 15" × 20".
5. Two trash containers (one for paper, one for trash) are each 14" × 18" × 21" tall.
6. Cash drawer below register is 15" wide with a 6" tall drawer face.
7. Supplies drawer 15" wide × 6" tall.
8. Additional closed storage where possible with one adjustable shelf per unit.
9. Label all finishes/surface materials for the desk; note incremental and overall dimensions.
10. Indicate with hidden lines and a note the barrier-free transaction surface at 30" high.
11. Draw and note a second transaction surface at 45" high.

Electrical Plan

1. Review the requirements on sheet P2-2 and provide for all required devices.

Lighting/Reflected Ceiling Plan

1. Energy conservation to be balanced with effective lighting techniques in display and sales area.
2. Solution to be safe and conform with codes.

Use the space below to draw (to scale) your design for the sales desk showing all equipment devices, dimensions, and material descriptions.

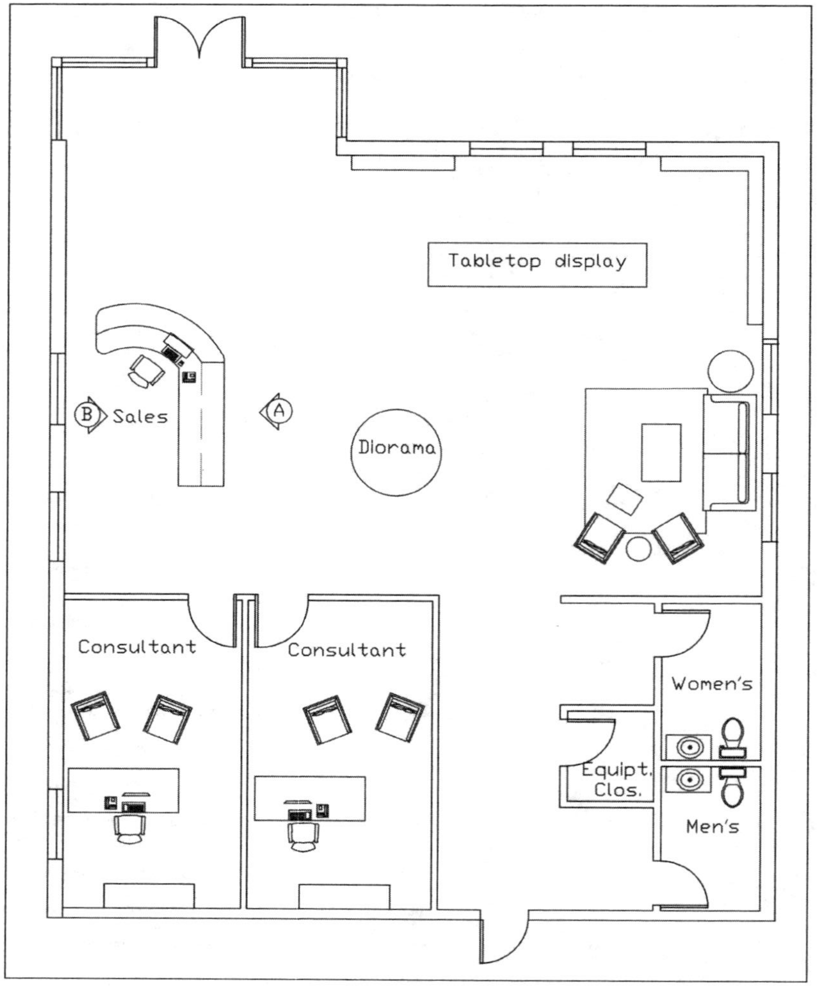

Timed Design Exercise

Part 2 of 2

Floor Plan
Weaver's Studio, Lite Version

Sheet **P2-1**

Scale: 1/8" = 1'-0"

Control Number

Tabletop display

Diorama

Women's

Men's

Equipt. Clos.

Consultant

Consultant

Sales

Ⓐ Elevation of Customer Side of Sales Desk
Scale: 1/4" = 1'-0"

Ⓑ Elevation of Staff Side of Sales Desk
Scale: 1/4" = 1'-0"

Electrical/Data/Phone Plan
Weaver's Studio, Lite Version

Sheet **P2-2**

Scale   1/8" = 1'-0"

Control Number

Electrical Legend

	Duplex outlet
GFI	Ground Fault Interrupt duplex outlet
	Quadruplex outlet
	220-volt outlet
	Cat 3 phone port
	Cat 5 data port
	Phone and data port
	Phone/data/power
	Floor duplex outlet
	Floor phone port
	Floor data port

Use only these symbols to communicate your design. Do not make up your own symbols.

Equipment List
Note all heights that deviate from typical 18" AFF

Qty	Location and requirements
1	Sales desk: phone/data/power in desktop
1	Sales desk: one phone line 24" AFF
1	Diorama: duplex in floor under pedestal
1	Advisor desk: phone/data/power each office
1	Advisor desk: phone each office
2	Equipt closet: phone/data/power closet
2	Equipment closet: quadruplex outlet closet
2	Display shelving wall: duplex outlets 45" AFF
1	Washroom one GFI outlet at sink in each restroom

Refer to this list as you prepare your electrical/data/power plan; select and show only these items on that plan.

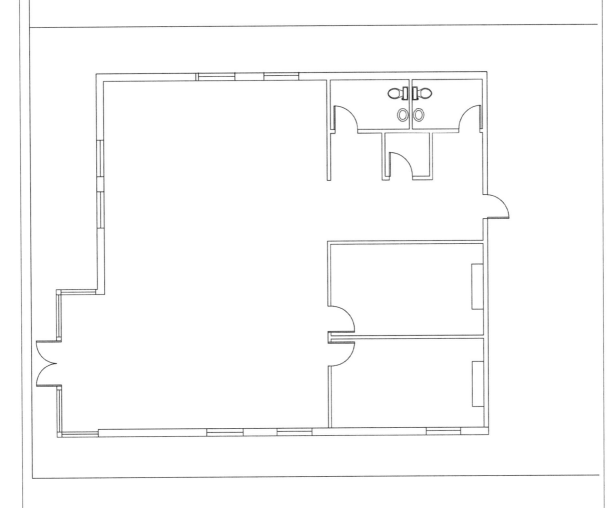

Weaver's Studio, Lite Version   **Timed Design Exercises**   Part 2 of 2   **CD**

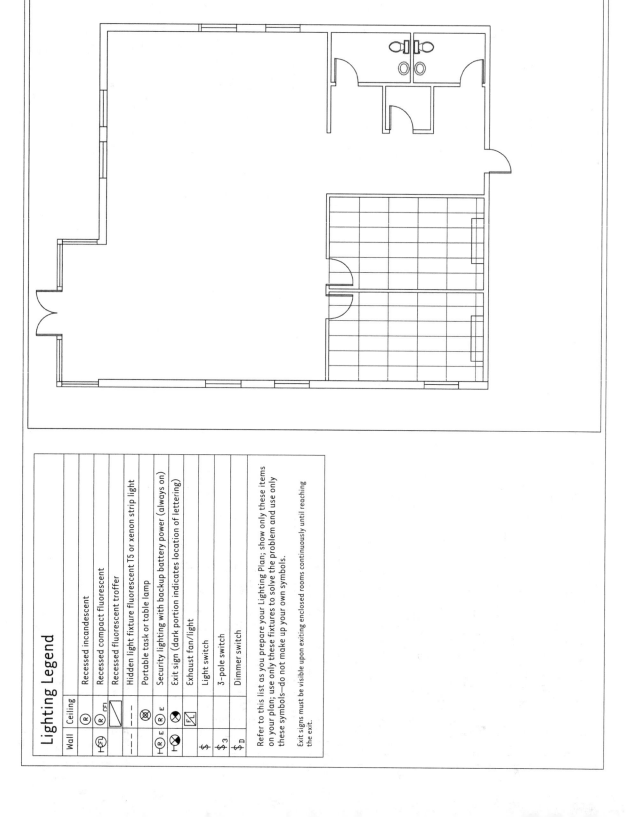

Timed Design
Exercise

Part 2 of 2

Reflected Ceiling Plan
Weaver's Studio, Lite Version

Sheet   P2-3

Scale   1/8" = 1'-0"

Control Number

Lighting Legend

Wall	Ceiling	
	®	Recessed incandescent
⊢Ⓕ	®OFl	Recessed compact fluorescent
	▱	Recessed fluorescent troffer
– – –	– – –	Hidden light fixture fluorescent T5 or xenon strip light
	⊗	Portable task or table lamp
⊢® E	® E	Security lighting with backup battery power (always on)
⊢⊗	⊗	Exit sign (dark portion indicates location of lettering)
	⊠ FL	Exhaust fan/light
⌐$		Light switch
⌐$₃		3-pole switch
⌐$D		Dimmer switch

Refer to this list as you prepare your Lighting Plan; show only these items on your plan; use only these fixtures to solve the problem and use only these symbols—do not make up your own symbols.

Exit signs must be visible upon exiting enclosed rooms continuously until reaching the exit.

DESIGN SCENARIO 2

Coffee Shop, Full Version

COFFEE SHOP

Full Version (131 points total)

Suggested Scoring Part One

The following *must* be met for 5 points:

____ Living functions are not intermingled with studio functions.

____ Paths of travel from studio function do not have visual contact with living functions other than entry and powder room functions.

____ Safe egress is available to both functional spaces.

____ Floor drains within 8 feet of pipe locations.

(20 points)

The following *must* be met for 2 points each:

____ Egress is not blocked, locked, or used for storage.

____ Paths of egress are barrier free and are a minimum of 44 inches wide.

____ The entrance, studio, and restroom are barrier free.

____ The family can exit the residence more than one way.

____ Doors along paths of exit travel are 36 inches wide and do not impinge upon clear 44-inch-wide path.

____ Open storage does not impinge on 44-inch-wide clear paths of exit travel.

____ Doors that are not along an exit path of travel are at least 30 inches clear open width.

____ Accessible doors have 18 inches clear wall space on the pull side of the latch edge and 12 inches on the pull side of the hinge edge.

____ Door swings do not encroach on turning circles.

____ Habitable spaces have natural light and ventilation.

____ The artists using the residence's powder room do not travel through rooms other than the entry in the residence.

____ Plumbing locations are within 12 feet of plumbing stacks.

____ Exterior openings are used for new windows and doors; none are added and none taken away.

____ Family bathroom is adjacent to bedrooms and is separate from powder room.

____ Entrance serves studio and residence equally.

____ Location contributes to sound separation.

____ Bedrooms have reasonable fire-escape options.

____ Solution is correctly portrayed entirely on sheet P1-2.

____ Adjacency matrix is complete and correct.

(38 points)

The following *must* to be shown on matrix and floor plan for 1 point each:

____ Direct adjacency BRs to Family Bath

____ Direct adjacency Powder Room to Entrance

____ Direct adjacency Kitchen to Dining

____ Convenient adjacency Entrance to Studio

____ Convenient adjacency Entertainment to Powder Room

____ Material schedule
Entrance floor F-2 walls W-4
Studio floor F-1 walls W-1
Editing Room floor F-4 walls W-2
Powder Restroom floor F-2 walls W-3

(6 points)

The following *should* be met for additional ½ point each:

Recording Studio

Mixing Room

____ Fifteen LF work surface measured along inside edge, not the wall edge.

____ Two executive chairs

____ Double-pane glass

Soundproof Studio

____ Less than 20 feet and more than 10 feet in each direction

____ 12-inch-thick walls all around

Editing Room

____ 20 LF U-shaped work surface with chair

____ Double pedestal desk with chair

Entrance

___ Eight LF coat storage

___ 36 inches × 20 inches set-down surface

Living Room

___ Lounge seating for eight

___ Set-down surface at each seat

___ Shelving minimum 6 feet wide × 2 feet deep

___ 5 foot widescreen TV indicated

___ Seating oriented for conversation

Dining Area

___ Table seating for 6 to 10 (extension table or other solution indicated)

___ Buffet 8 feet long

Kitchen

___ 15 LF of base and 10 LF of uppers

___ Refrigerator 30 inches × 28 inches × 72 inches tall

___ Dishwasher 2 feet × 2 feet

___ Microwave 21 inches wide × 18 inches deep

___ Sink 24 inches × 18 inches

Master Bedroom

___ King-size bed with minimum 2 feet clearance on each side

___ Nightstands 24 inches wide × 20 inches deep (from front to back) with clear space to access drawers below

___ Dresser 7 feet wide × 20 inches deep

___ Closet 16 feet LF of hanging

___ Desk 6 feet × 2$\frac{1}{2}$ feet

___ TV with 40-inch-wide flatscreen indicated

___ Seating for conversation or TV

Child Bedroom

___ Twin bed

___ Surface near bed for clock and lamp

___ Dresser 4 feet wide and 20 inches deep

___ Closet with 5 LF hanging minimum

___ Desk 5 feet wide × 2$\frac{1}{2}$ inches deep with chair

___ Accommodates one sleepover guest

Family Bathroom

___ Vanity 60 inches wide × 22 inches deep

___ Two sinks

___ Toilet and tub

___ Linen closet

(19 points)

The following *must* be present for 1 point each:

___ No item of furniture taller than 3 feet should be placed in front of windows with 3-foot-high sill

___ All required items are illustrated or labeled to differentiate from other item types

(2 points)

Suggested Scoring Part Two

The following *should* be met for 2 points each:

___ Plans are completed using only the selections and symbols given

___ Outlets are noted at 18 inches AFF except for the sales desk outlets and devices

___ Exit signage positioned for visibility from all locations (except inside washroom)

___ Outlets are wall outlets wherever practical, including eight laptop outlet locations

(8 points)

Desk Elevations

The following *should* be met for 2 points each:

___ The desk is accurately sketched or drafted to scale as required by elevation markers

___ The staff side indicates with symbols or notes phone and supply drawer

___ The refrigerator and pastry cases are show with display on customer side and sliding doors on staff side

___ Staff side has two trash containers conveniently located; each is 14 inches × 18 inches × 21 inches

___ Drawer space 24 inches wide (aggregate), 6 inches tall

___ Materials are noted

___ Sufficient dimensions to comprehend design, locations for services, and storage and size of storage spaces

(14 points)

Electrical Plan

The following *should* be met for 1 point each:

Service Counter

___ Voice/data/power

___ Phone

___ Back service counter GFI 40 inches AFF at sink

Coffee Shop

___ Recessed outlet on art wall

___ Eight convenience outlets for laptops

Kitchen

___ Voice/data/power for flat-panel display

___ Duplex 34-inch AFF cook's desk

___ Voice/data/power cook's desk

Washroom

___ GFI at sink

___ Hand drier

(10 points)

Lighting Plan

Each of the following *should* be shown for 1 point each:

___ Fluorescent lights for ambient light

___ Flexible track for performance lighting

___ Exit signage visible from all locations in shop (outside of restroom)

___ Minimum seven light fixtures in seating/performance area

___ Minimum one light fixture in restroom

___ Minimum one light fixture in hallway

___ Minimum four light fixtures in kitchen

___ Each incandescent lamp or 1 foot of incandescent strip = 2, and each fluorescent lamp and exit light = 1; total not to exceed 40

___ Fan/light in bathroom

___ Emergency lighting incorporated into scheme

___ Task lighting provided at sales counter

___ Task light at cook's desk

___ Light arranged for shadowless work surface in kitchen

___ Lighting controls properly communicated

(14 points)

Timed Design Exercise

Part 1 of 2

Part One of Design Exercise
Coffee Shop, Full Version

Sheet

C-1

Scale   None

Student Control Number

TIMED DESIGN EXERCISE

Instructions to Students

1. Read all of these instructions before beginning the exercise.
2. Review the project and code requirements as well as the site plan P1-1.
3. Review the floor plan P1-2.
4. Review the matrix, material options, and material schedules.
5. Review the interior elevation showing the window fenestration from the interior P1-1.
6. Read the entire project description and carefully review the requirements in each area.
7. Complete the adjacency matrix P1-1.
8. Show your proposed layout on sheet P1-2 to solve the problem defined (following).
9. Select finish materials for the floors and walls, and indicate the best choice by circling it on the schedule P1-1.
10. Write your control number in the lower right of every sheet—even the ones that you don't write on.

Code Requirements

- All exterior doors are available for egress (an exit required per code) and are shown as out-swinging doors that have a minimum clear opening of 3'.
- Egress paths of travel may not pass through areas that may be blocked, locked, or used for storage.
- Barrier free requires a 5' turning circle (show as a dotted line) at every change in direction. Paths of travel not required to be barrier free are not bound by this restriction.
- The entry serves the residence and recording studio. The recording studio and path of travel from the recording studio to the guest powder room in the residence must be barrier free.
- Maintain a minimum width of 44" along accessible routes. Doors and storage units that open toward a path of travel may not limit the clear passage width when open.
- Doors to be a minimum of 3' clear width in all accessible spaces and a minimum 30" clear width otherwise. Doors in accessible areas must be flanked by clear wall space 18" on the pull side and 12" wide on the push side along the latching side.
- Sinks in barrier-free areas must have clear knee space below and may not encroach on the turning circle more than 6".
- Habitable spaces in the living space/apartment must have an operable window.
- Flooring in areas with sinks must be slip resistant.
- Surfaces in bathrooms and washrooms must be moisture resistant.

Design Requirements

All items, adjacencies, and attributes mentioned in this document are required in your passing solution. Use a freehand sketch or drafting to represent items in accurate scale. Draw your solution on drawing sheets provided using ink or felt tip (it will be assumed that all pencil is preliminary to your final solution and not intended as part of your final solution). You need only erase pencil marks that will interfere with comprehension of your solution.

Complete the partition and furniture plan on P1-1, showing typical required details (door swings, backs on chairs, pillows on bed, etc.) to the extent necessary to distinguish one type of item from another. Label on the plan all spaces listed in the project description. Include the lineal feet or cubic feet of storage required with the label for such items where the specific requirement is noted on the project requirements list.

Project Description

The owner of this residence with an attached coffee shop promotes musicians and poets with performance space in the coffee shop and a small recording studio in her residence. Her family of three includes her spouse and her 6-year-old son.

Requirements for each functional area follow. Address the items to be represented as well as adjacencies and privacy considerations. Functions may be combined as long as all requirements are met.

Plumbing locations should be within 12' radius of existing plumbing locations, which are noted as circles for waste and supplies on the plan on P1-2. The building shell with windows and doors as indicated cannot be changed. This converted warehouse will have the garage doors on the south facade replaced with glass (clear or frosted as will suit your solution). The clerestory windows on the east and west facades rise from 10' to 13' AFF (above finished floor) and are operated by a motor or manually. The windows overlooking the service alley on the north side are double-hung (operable and available for emergency fire exit as well as ventilation) and rise from 30" AFF to 96" AFF.

Recording Function

1. Soundproof studio with walls on all 4 sides shown 12" thick. This room is to be a rectangular room with a minimum depth of 10' and a maximum width of 20'; it is to be accessed from the mixing room.
2. Mixing room with a minimum of 15 lineal feet desk-height counter surface and two executive desk chairs. This room is to have direct visual connection to the recording room via a laminated, double-pane fixed glass panel.
3. An editing room/office with a U-shaped workstation having a minimum of 20 lineal feet measured along interior/work side of desk-height counter surface.

Double-file pedestal desk with a computer for a separate business function. Each of these desks must have its own chair.

The recording studio shares an entrance with the residence. The guest powder room in the residence is used by the people working and recording in the studio. Other than this access, the studio is to be as separate from the residence as possible for sound and convenience for the family space, as recording sessions can sometimes go late into the night.

Living Space/Apartment

Entrance
1. 8 lineal feet of coat closet
2. 3 lineal feet × 20" deep set-down surface
3. Adjacent to recording studio entrance and also conveniently serving residence

This area serves both the recording studio and the residence and should also serve as a divider between them.

Living Room
1. Lounge seating for eight configured for conversation or TV
2. A surface to set things down at each seat
3. Shelving unit containing TV and stereo equipment measuring at least 6' wide × 2' deep
4. Widescreen TV that can be conveniently viewed from the seating; allow 5' of width for TV screen.

Dining
1. Table and chairs for 6 people (80" long) to 10 people (120" long)
2. Buffet surface 8' long with storage below

Kitchen
1. 15 lineal feet clear counter space over base cabinets and appliances
2. 10 lineal feet of upper cabinets
3. Full-height refrigerator 36" wide × 28" deep
4. Undercounter dishwasher 24" × 24"
5. Microwave 21" wide × 18" deep × 15" tall
6. Sink 24" wide × 18" deep from front to back
7. Range 30" wide × 28" deep from front to back

Guest Powder Room
1. Toilet
2. Sink

This room must be handicapped accessible and accessed by people working and recording in the studio along a limited travel path (to keep the residence as private as possible).

Master Bedroom
1. King-size bed 76" × 80"
2. Nightstand each side of bed 2' wide × 20" deep
3. Dresser 7' wide × 20" deep × 40" tall
4. Desk minimum 6' wide × 30" deep with desk chair
5. 16 lineal feet of hanging clothing storage
6. Lounge seating for two oriented for TV or conversation
7. Widescreen, flat-panel TV 40" wide

Child Sleep Space
1. Twin bed 39" wide × 75" long
2. Surface near bed for clock and lamp
3. Dresser 4' wide × 20" deep from front to back
4. Closet with 3' of long hanging and 4' of short/double hanging
5. Desk minimum 5' wide × 30" deep with chair
6. Accommodation for sleepover guest

Family Bathroom
1. Vanity cabinet 60" wide × 22" deep containing two sinks
2. Toilet
3. Tub 2'-6" wide × 5'-0" long with shower. Indicate location of fittings (shower head and faucet)
4. Linen closet 24" wide × 24" deep full height

Site Plan
Elevation
Matrix
Schedule
Coffee Shop, Full Version

Sheet   P1-1

Scale   As Noted

Control Number

Adjacency Matrix
Use only these symbols; do not make up your own symbols.

● Direct Adjacency
○ Convenient Adjacency
☐ Visual Connection
X Remote

	Sound Studio	Edit	Mixing Room	Entrance	Living Room	Dining Room	Kitchen	Master BR	Child BR	Guest Bath	Family Bath
Sound Studio											
Edit											
Mixing Room											
Entrance											
Living Room											
Dining Room											
Kitchen											
Master BR											
Child BR											
Guest Bath											
Family Bath											

F	Floor
F1	45 oz level loop nylon carpet tiles loose lay
F2	Stained concrete sealed 3 coats matte nonslip urethane
F3	Unguaged slate with heavy cleft face acrylic high-gloss sealer
F4	Recycled rubber tiles w/ antistatic additives
F5	Linoleum sheet goods
W	Walls
W1	Textile wall covering
W2	Semigloss, low VOC paint
W3	Ceramic tile
W4	Textured commercial vinyl wall covering

Circle the most appropriate choice from those listed to the right by referencing the table above for material descriptions.

Area	Floor			Walls		
Entrance	F1	F2	F5	W1	W3	W4
Studio	F1	F2	F3	W1	W2	W3
Edit Room	F3	F4	F5	W1	W2	W3
Powder Room	F1	F2	F3	W1	W2	W3

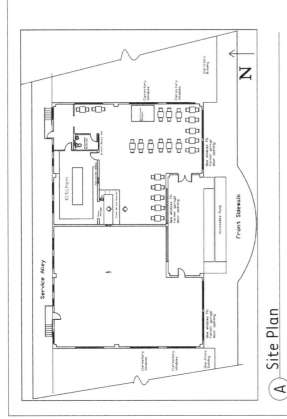

A) Site Plan

B) Exterior Elevation South Facade
Scale 1/16" = 1'-0"

C) Exterior Elevation East Facade
Scale 1/16" = 1'-0"

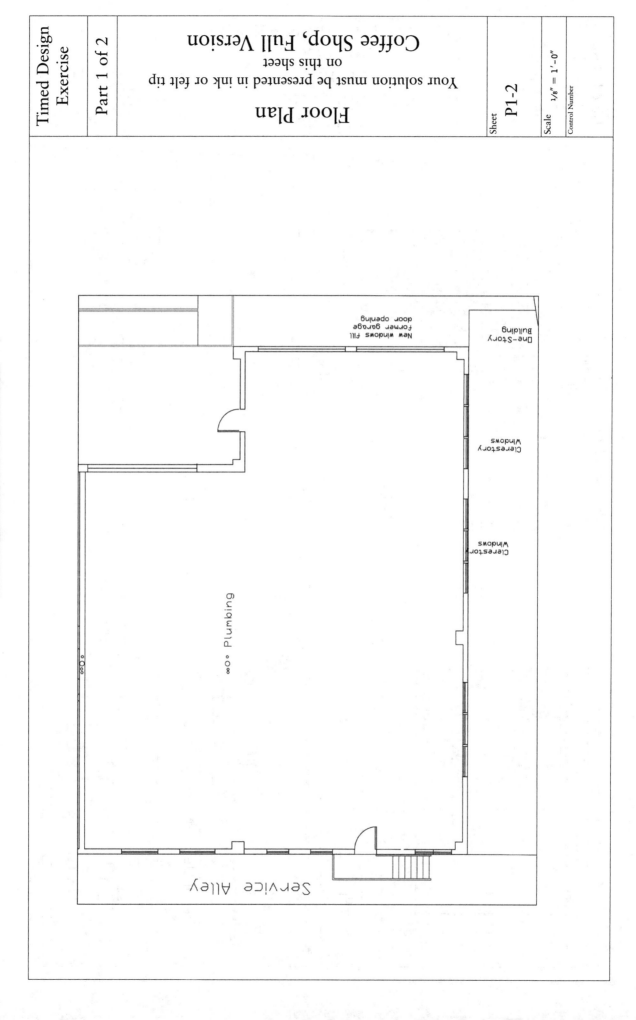

Timed Design Exercise

Part 1 of 2

Coffee Shop, Full Version
on this sheet
Your solution must be presented in ink or felt tip

Floor Plan

Sheet P1-2

Scale 1/8" = 1'-0"

Control Number

Plumbing

New windows fill
Former garage
door opening

One-Story Building

Clerestory Windows

Clerestory Windows

Service Alley

TIMED DESIGN EXERCISE

Part Two of Design Exercise
Coffee Shop, Full Version

Generic form of refrigerator and pastry cabinets

Instructions to Students

1. Read all of these instructions before beginning the exercise.
2. Review the project and code requirements and additional scope of services.
3. Review the floor plan P2-1; notice the layout for your lighting and electrical planning and also the elevation symbols indicating the two elevations for the sales counter, which are to be drawn on sheet P2-1 at 1/4" = 1'0" (requirements follow).
4. Review all of the symbols and electrical requirements on sheet P2-2.
5. Locate the electrical and communication devices required on the electrical/data/phone plan, sheet P2-2.
6. Create a reflected ceiling plan on sheet P2-3 showing all lighting locations.
7. Draw required circuitry and switching locations for a functional design.
8. Write your control number where indicated in the lower right corner of every sheet—even the ones that you don't write on.
9. Select the best choice from the equipment listed in the legends and use only that equipment and those symbols. Do not add equipment or make up your own symbols.
10. Review P2-1 and note the location for elevations of the sales desk.

Code Requirements

- All electrical outlets must be located 18" AFF unless noted otherwise.
- Exit signage must be continuously visible along paths of travel toward exit to the outside.
- Where practical, wall outlets and ports are preferred over floor-mounted outlets and ports.
- Electricity, voice, and data devices required at the sales desk are to be brought up into and permanently affixed within the sales counter.

Additional Scope of Services

The coffee shop serves coffee and sandwiches and attracts customers for evening performances by musicians, poets, and performance artists. Coffee drinks are made to order at the service counter. Food items are to be displayed in a pastry cabinet and a refrigerator cabinet, which are part of the service counter. A menu of made-to-order sandwiches and salads is displayed on the wall above the service counter. These orders are relayed electronically to the kitchen when the sale is rung up. Orders are delivered through a pass-through window from the kitchen to the service counter. Coffee is brewed and orders are assembled and wrapped at the back portion of the service counter.

Food items are packaged "to go" and may be carried away or eaten in the shop. Catering of sandwich-based meals is also available from the kitchen. Catering customers sometimes pick up orders at the service counter.

A small performance platform with flexible lighting serves a variety of small performances, including poetry and storytelling, musicians' performances, and performance art. An industrial atmosphere is requested.

Design Requirements

All items, adjacencies, and attributes mentioned in this document are required in your solution. Use a freehand sketch or drafting to represent items in accurate scale. Draw your solution on drawing sheets provided using ink or felt tip (it will be assumed that all pencil is preliminary to your final solution and not intended as part of your final solution).

Project Description

Service Counter—Front Counter

1. The sales counter will include two floor-standing food-display cases that are each 4' wide × 30" deep × 45" tall.
2. The refrigerator case houses a condenser in its 2' tall base. The pastry cabinet has concealed storage in its 2' high base. The upper portion of each case is 1/2" thick acrylic on the customer side and enameled steel sliding doors on the staff side.
3. A computerized cash register sits on the sales counter 36" AFF and is networked to a flat-panel display in the kitchen. The jack that connects and powers the register is to be located 24" AFF in a closed-door storage unit within the service counter, below the computer.
4. A phone is also located on the counter next to the register.
5. Drawer space for supplies to be aggregately (need not be a single drawer) 24" wide with a 6" tall drawer face and 10" deep with full-extension glides.
6. Indicate on the plan view with hidden lines and a note the barrier-free transaction surface at 30" high.
7. Two identical trash and paper refuse bins are each 14" × 18" × 31" tall.
8. Note materials to be used.

The back service counter is not part of the design tasks for this exercise.

Electrical Plan

1. Review the requirements on sheet P2-2 and provide for all required devices.

Lighting/Reflected Ceiling Plan

1. Energy conservation to be balanced with effective lighting techniques in performance, dining, and sales areas.
2. Solution to be safe and conform with codes.

Coffee Shop, Full Version | Timed Design Exercises | Part 2 of 2 CD

Timed Design Exercise

Part 2 of 2

Floor Plan
Coffee Shop, Full Version

Sheet
P2-1

Scale: 1/8" = 1'-0"

Control Number

Use the space below to draw (to scale) your design for the service counter showing all equipment devices, dimensions, and material descriptions.

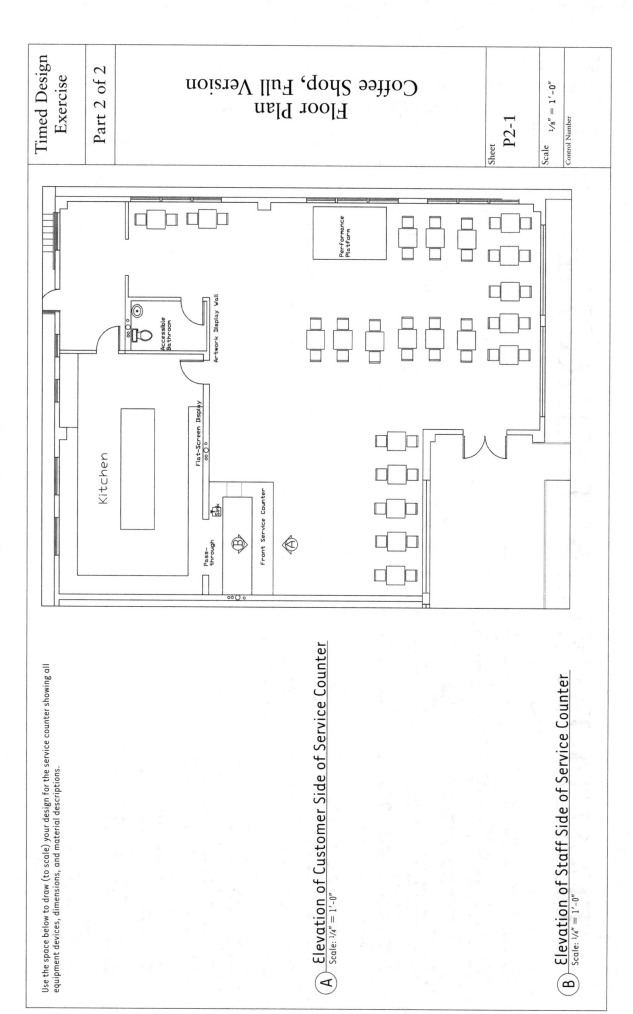

A Elevation of Customer Side of Service Counter
Scale: 1/4" = 1'-0"

B Elevation of Staff Side of Service Counter
Scale: 1/4" = 1'-0"

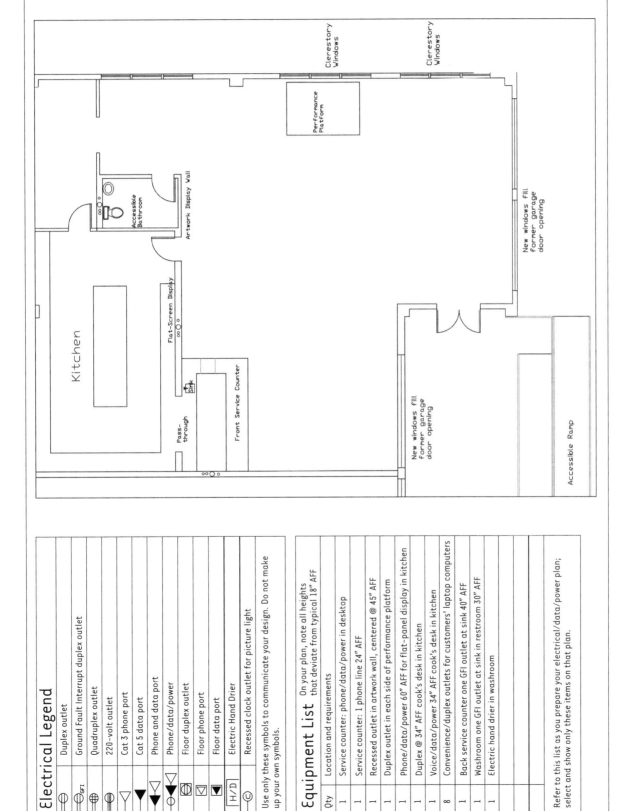

Timed Design Exercise

Part 2 of 2

Electrical/Data/Phone Plan
Coffee Shop, Full Version

Sheet **P2-2**

Scale

Control Number

Electrical Legend

	Duplex outlet
GFI	Ground Fault Interrupt duplex outlet
	Quadruplex outlet
	220-volt outlet
	Cat 3 phone port
▼	Cat 5 data port
▽	Phone and data port
▼	Phone/data/power
	Floor duplex outlet
▽	Floor phone port
▼	Floor data port
H/D	Electric Hand Drier
	Recessed clock outlet for picture light

Use only these symbols to communicate your design. Do not make up your own symbols.

Equipment List
On your plan, note all heights that deviate from typical 18" AFF

Qty	Location and requirements
1	Service counter: phone/data/power in desktop
1	Service counter: 1 phone line 24" AFF
1	Recessed outlet in artwork wall, centered @ 45" AFF
1	Duplex outlet in each side of performance platform
1	Phone/data/power 60" AFF for flat-panel display in kitchen
1	Duplex @ 34" AFF cook's desk in kitchen
1	Voice/data/power 34" AFF cook's desk in kitchen
8	Convenience/duplex outlets for customers' laptop computers
1	Back service counter one GFI outlet at sink 40" AFF
1	Washroom one GFI outlet at sink in restroom 30" AFF
1	Electric hand drier in washroom

Refer to this list as you prepare your electrical/data/power plan; select and show only these items on that plan.

83

Design Scenario 2

Coffee Shop, Full Version | **Timed Design Exercises** | Part 2 of 2 | **CD**

Timed Design Exercise	
Part 2 of 2	

Reflected Ceiling Plan
Coffee Shop, Full Version

Sheet	**P2-3**
Scale ⅛" = 1'-0"	
Control Number	

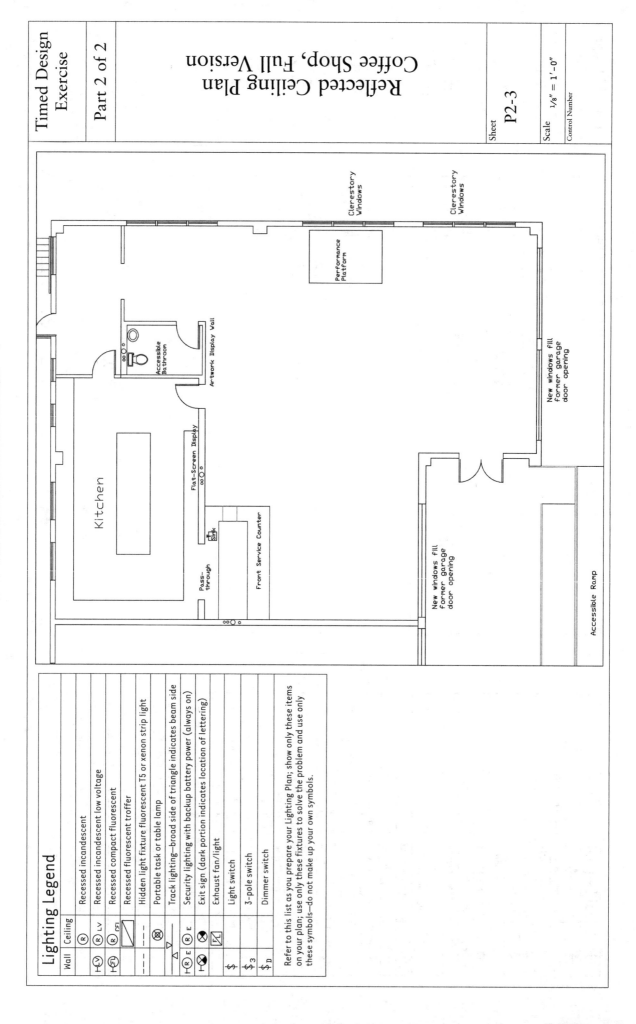

Lighting Legend

Wall	Ceiling	
	®	Recessed incandescent
⊢®⊣ LV	® LV	Recessed incandescent low voltage
⊢®⊣	® nFl	Recessed compact fluorescent
	▱	Recessed fluorescent troffer
— — —	— — —	Hidden light fixture fluorescent T5 or xenon strip light
	⊗	Portable task or table lamp
▷	▷	Track lighting—broad side of triangle indicates beam side
⊢® E ⊣	® E	Security lighting with backup battery power (always on)
⊗	⊗	Exit sign (dark portion indicates location of lettering)
	⊠	Exhaust fan/light
$		Light switch
$₃		3-pole switch
$D		Dimmer switch

Refer to this list as you prepare your Lighting Plan; show only these items on your plan; use only these fixtures to solve the problem and use only these symbols—do not make up your own symbols.

Kitchen

Accessible Bathroom

Artwork Display Wall

Flat-Screen Display

Pass-through

Front Service Counter

Sink

Performance Platform

Clerestory Windows

Clerestory Windows

New windows fill former garage door opening

New windows fill former garage door opening

Accessible Ramp

DESIGN SCENARIO 2

Coffee Shop, Lite Version

COFFEE SHOP

Lite Version (116 points total)

Suggested Scoring Part One

The following *must* be met for 5 points:

___ Living functions are not intermingled with studio functions.

___ Paths of travel from studio function do not have visual contact with living functions other than entry and powder room functions.

___ Safe egress is available to both functional spaces.

___ All plumbing is within 12 feet of stacks.

(20 points)

The following *must* be met for 2 points each:

___ Egress is not blocked, locked, or used for storage.

___ Paths of egress are barrier free and are a minimum of 44 inches wide.

___ The entrance, studio, and restroom are barrier free.

___ The family can exit the residence more than one way.

___ Doors along paths of exit travel are 36 inches wide and do not impinge upon clear 44-inch-wide path.

___ Open storage does not impinge on 44-inch-wide clear paths of exit travel.

___ Doors that are not along an exit path of travel are at least 30 inches clear open width.

___ Accessible doors have 18 inches clear wall space on the pull side of the latch edge and 12 inches on the pull side of the hinge edge.

___ Door swings do not encroach on turning circles.

___ Habitable spaces have natural light and ventilation.

___ The artists using the residence powder room do not travel through rooms other than the entry in the residence.

___ Exterior openings are used for new windows and doors; none are added and none taken away.

___ Entrance serves recording and residence function equally.

___ Bedroom has safe fire-escape options.

___ Solution is correctly portrayed entirely on sheet P1-2.

___ Adjacency matrix is complete and correct.

(32 points)

The following *should* be shown on matrix and plan for 1 point each:

___ Direct adjacency BRs to Bath

___ Direct adjacency Powder Room to Entrance

___ Direct adjacency Kitchen to Dining

___ Convenient adjacency Entrance to Studio

___ Convenient adjacency Entertainment to Powder Room

___ Material schedule
Entrance floor F-2 walls W-4
Studio floor F-1 walls W-1
Editing Room floor F-4 walls W-2
Powder Restroom floor F-2 walls W-3

(6 points)

The following *should* be met for additional ¹/₂ point each:

Recording Studio

Mixing Room

___ 10 LF work surface measured along inside edge

___ Two chairs

___ Double-pane glass indicated

Soundproof Studio

___ Minimum 7 feet × 12 feet

___ 12-inch-thick walls all around

Editing Room

___ 10 LF L or U-shaped work surface with chair

___ 6 LF of desk surface for assistant

___ Assistant work surface has file pedestal and assistant has a chair

Entrance

___ 5 LF coat storage

___ 36 inches × 20 inches set-down surface

Living Area

Living Room

___ Lounge seating for six

___ Set-down surface at each seat

___ Shelving minimum 6 feet wide × 2 feet deep

___ 5 foot widescreen TV indicated

___ Arranged for TV or conversation

Dining Area

___ Table seating for six

Kitchen

___ 15 LF of base and 10 LF of uppers

___ Refrigerator 30 inches × 28 inches × 72 inches tall

___ Dishwasher 2 feet × 2 feet

___ Sink 24 inches × 18 inches

___ Range 30 inches wide × 28 inches deep from front to back

___ Upper cabinets indicated

Master Bedroom

___ King-size bed with minimum 2 feet clearance on each side

___ Set-down surface next to both sides of bed

___ Dresser 7 feet wide × 20 inches deep; may function as bedside surfaces

___ Closet 10 feet LF of hanging

___ Desk 6 feet × 2½ feet

Bathroom

___ Vanity 60 inches wide × 22 inches deep

___ Toilet

___ Tub (2½ feet × 5 feet)

___ Linen closet

One point for each of the following:

___ No item of furniture taller than 3 feet should be placed in front of windows with 3-foot-high sill

___ All required items are illustrated or labeled to differentiate from other item types

___ Flow and logic prevail over choppy and cluttered layout

(17 points)

Suggested Scoring Part Two

The following *should* be met for 2 points each:

___ Plans are completed using only the selections and symbols given

___ Outlets are noted at 18 inches AFF Typ, unless required to be otherwise

___ Exit signage positioned for visibility from all locations (except inside washroom)

___ Outlets are wall outlets wherever practical, including eight laptop outlet locations

(8 points)

Desk Elevations

The following *should* be met for 2 points each:

___ The desk is accurately sketched or drafted to scale as required by elevation markers

___ The staff side indicates phone and supply drawer with symbols or notes

___ Staff side has two trash containers conveniently located; each is 14 inches × 18 inches × 21 inches

___ Drawer space 24 inches wide (aggregate), 6 inches tall

___ Materials are noted

___ Sufficient dimensions to comprehend design, locations for services, storage, and size of storage spaces

(12 points)

Electrical Plan

The following *should* be met for 1 point each:

Service Counter

___ Voice/data/power

___ Phone

___ Back service counter GFI 40 inches AFF at sink

Coffee Shop

___ Recessed outlet on art wall

___ Eight convenience outlets for laptops

Kitchen

___ Voice/data/power for flat-panel display

___ Duplex 34-inch AFF cook's desk

___ Voice/data/power cook's desk

Washroom

___ GFI at sink

___ Hand drier

Lighting Plan

____ Fluorescent lights for ambient light

____ Flexible track for performance lighting

____ Exit signage visible from all locations in shop (outside of restroom)

____ Minimum seven light fixtures in seating/performance area

____ Minimum one light fixture in restroom

____ Minimum one light fixture in hallway

____ Minimum four light fixtures in kitchen

(17 points)

One point awarded for:

____ Fan/light in bathroom

____ Emergency lighting incorporated into scheme

____ Task lighting provided at sales counter and cook's desk

____ Each incandescent lamp and foot of incandescent strip used multiplied by 2, plus each fluorescent and exit light multiplied by 1, should not add up to more than 50

(4 points)

TIMED DESIGN EXERCISE

Instructions to Students

1. Read all of these instructions before beginning the exercise.
2. Review the project and code requirements as well as the site plan P1-1.
3. Review the floor plan P1-2.
4. Review the matrix, material options, and material schedules.
5. Review the interior elevation showing the window fenestration from the interior P1-1.
6. Read the entire project description and carefully review the requirements in each area.
7. Complete the adjacency matrix P1-1.
8. Show your proposed layout on sheet P1-2 to solve the problem defined (following).
9. Select finish materials for the floors and walls and indicate the best choice for the schedule P1-1.
10. Write your control number in the lower right of every sheet—even the ones that you don't write on.

Code Requirements

- All exterior doors are available for egress (an exit required per code) and are shown as out-swinging doors that have a minimum clear opening of 3'.
- Egress paths of travel may not pass through areas that may be blocked, locked, or used for storage.
- Barrier free requires a 5' turning circle (show as a dotted line) at every change in direction. Paths of travel not required to be barrier free are not bound by this restriction.
- The entry serves the residence and recording studio. The recording studio and path of travel from the recording studio to the guest powder room in the residence must be barrier free.
- Maintain a minimum width of 44" along accessible routes. Doors and storage units that open toward a path of travel may not limit the clear passage width when open.
- Doors to be a minimum of 3' clear width in all accessible spaces and a minimum 30" clear width otherwise. Doors in accessible areas must be flanked by clear wall space 18" on the pull side and 12" wide on the push side along the latching side.
- Sinks in barrier-free areas must have clear knee space below and may not encroach on the turning circle more than 6".
- Habitable spaces in the living space/apartment must have an operable window.
- Flooring in areas with sinks must be slip resistant.
- Surfaces in bathrooms and washrooms must be moisture resistant.

Design Requirements

All items, adjacencies, and attributes mentioned in this document are required in your passing solution. Use a freehand sketch or drafting to represent items in accurate scale. Draw your solution on drawing sheets provided using ink or felt tip (it will be assumed that all pencil is preliminary to your final solution and not intended as part of your final solution). You need only erase pencil marks that will interfere with comprehension of your solution.

Complete the partition and furniture plan on P1-1 showing typical required details (door swings, backs on chairs, pillows on bed, etc.) to the extent necessary to distinguish one type of item from another. Label on the plan all spaces listed in the project description. Include the lineal feet or cubic feet of storage required with the label for such items where the specific requirement is noted on the project requirements list.

Project Description

The owner of this residence with an attached coffee shop promotes musicians and poets with performance space in the coffee shop and a small recording studio in her residence. Her family of three includes her spouse and her 6-year-old son.

Requirements for each functional area follow. Address the items to be represented as well as adjacencies and privacy considerations. Functions may be combined as long as all requirements are met.

Plumbing locations should be within a 12' radius of existing plumbing locations, which are noted as circles for waste and supplies on the plan on P1-2. The building shell with windows and doors as indicated cannot be changed. This converted warehouse will have the garage doors on the south facade replaced with glass (clear or frosted as will suit your solution). The clerestory windows on the east and west facades rise from 10' to 13' AFF (above finished floor) and are operated by a motor or manually. The windows overlooking the service alley on the north side are double-hung (operable and available for emergency fire exit as well as ventilation) rise from 30" AFF to 96" AFF.

Recording Function

1. Soundproof studio with walls on all 4 sides shown 12" thick. This room is to be 7' × 10' minimum and is to have direct visual connection to the mixing room via a large window.
2. Mixing room with a minimum of 10 lineal feet desk-height counter surface and an executive desk chair. This room is to have direct visual connection to the recording room via a laminated, double-pane fixed glass panel. Note window construction on plan.
3. An editing room/office with an L- or U-shaped workstation having a minimum of 10 lineal feet of counter measured along interior/work side of desk-height counter surface. A file pedestal desk area 6' wide with a computer for personal assistant is also to be in this area. Each of these work areas must have its own chair.

The recording studio shares an entrance with the residence. The guest powder room in the residence is used by the people working and recording in the studio. Other than this access, the studio is to be as separate from the residence as possible for sound and convenience for the family space, as recording sessions can sometimes go late into the night.

Living Space/Apartment

Entrance
1. 5 lineal feet of coat closet
2. 3 lineal feet × 20" deep set-down surface
3. Adjacent to recording studio entrance and also conveniently serving residence

This area serves both the recording studio and the residence and should also serve as a divider between them.

Living Room
1. Lounge seating for six configured for conversation or TV
2. A surface to set things down at each seat
3. Shelving unit containing TV and stereo equipment measuring at least 6' wide × 2' deep
4. Widescreen TV that can be conveniently viewed from the seating; allow 5' of width for TV screen.

Dining
1. Table and chairs for 6 people (80" long)
2. This function may be included in living room if an open plan is developed.

Kitchen
1. 15 lineal feet clear counter space over base cabinets and appliances
2. Upper cabinets where possible
3. Full-height refrigerator 36" wide × 28" deep
4. Undercounter dishwasher 24" × 24"
5. Range 30" wide × 28" deep from front to back
6. Sink 24" wide × 18" deep from front to back

Guest Powder Room
1. Toilet
2. Sink

This room must be handicapped accessible and accessed by people working and recording in the studio along a limited travel path (to keep the residence as private as possible).

Bedroom
1. King-size bed 76" × 80"
2. Set-down surface each side of bed
3. Dresser 7" wide × 20" deep from front to back
4. Desk minimum 6' wide × 30" deep with desk chair
5. 10 lineal feet of hanging clothing storage

Bathroom
1. Vanity cabinet 60" wide × 22" deep containing two sinks
2. Toilet
3. Tub 2'-6" wide × 5'-0" long with shower. Indicate location of fittings (shower head and faucet)
4. Linen closet 24" wide × 24" deep full height

Part One of Design Exercise
Coffee Shop, Lite Version

Timed Design Exercise

Part 1 of 2

Sheet **C-1**

Scale None

Student Control Number

Site Plan
Elevation
Matrix
Schedule
Coffee Shop, Lite Version

Sheet

P1-1

Scale   As Noted

Control Number

Adjacency Matrix
Use only these symbols; do not make up your own symbols.

● Direct Adjacency
○ Convenient Adjacency
X Remote

	Sound Studio	Edit/Mixing	Entrance	LR and DR	Kitchen	Bedroom	Bathroom
Sound Studio							
Edit/Mixing							
Entrance							
LR and DR							
Kitchen							
Bedroom							
Bathroom							

F	Floor
F1	45 oz level loop nylon carpet tiles loose lay
F2	Stained concrete sealed 3 coats matte nonslip urethane
F3	Ungauged slate with heavy cleft face acrylic high-gloss sealer
F4	Recycled rubber tiles size w/ antistatic additives
F5	Linoleum sheet goods
W	Walls
W1	Textile wall covering
W2	Semigloss, low VOC paint
W3	Ceramic tile
W4	Textured commercial vinyl wall covering

Circle the most appropriate choice from those listed to the right by referencing the table above for material descriptions.

Area	Floor			Walls		
Entrance	F1	F2	F4	W1	W3	W4
Studio	F1	F2	F3	W1	W2	W3
Edit/Mix	F1	F3	F4	W1	W3	W4
Bathroom	F1	F3	F2	W1	W2	W3

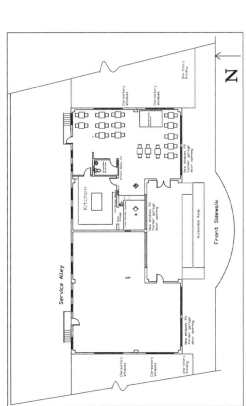

A Site Plan

B Exterior Elevation South Facade
Scale 1/16" = 1'-0"

C Exterior Elevation East Facade
Scale 1/16" = 1'-0"

Timed Design Exercise	Part 1 of 2	Coffee Shop, Lite Version

Your solution must be presented in ink or felt tip on this sheet

Floor Plan

Sheet	**P1-2**
Scale	1/8" = 1'-0"
Control Number	

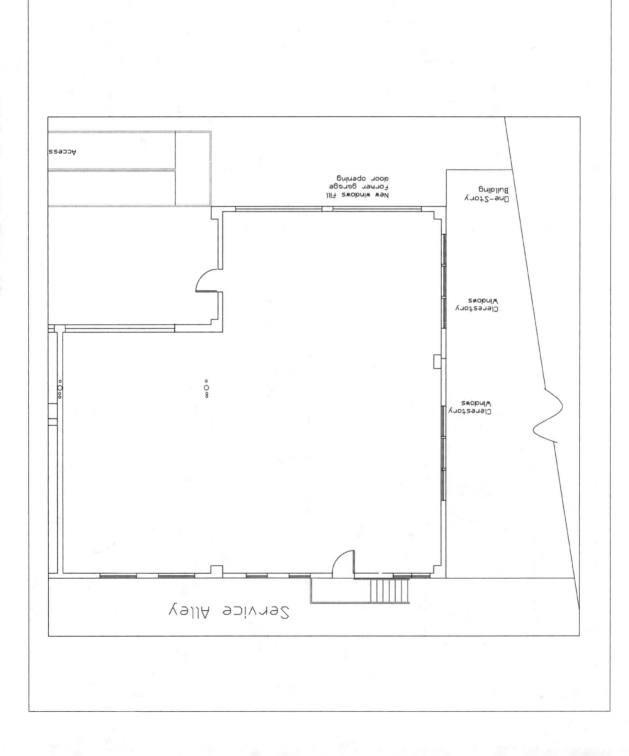

Access

New windows fill former garage door opening

One-Story Building

Clerestory Windows

Clerestory Windows

Service Alley

TIMED DESIGN EXERCISE

Timed Design Exercise

Part 2 of 2

Part Two of Design Exercise
Coffee Shop, Lite Version

Sheet

C-2

Scale None

Student Control Number

Instructions to Students

1. Read all of these instructions before beginning the exercise.
2. Review the project and code requirements and additional scope of services.
3. Review the floor plan P2-1, notice the layout for your lighting and electrical planning and also the elevation symbols indicating the two elevations for the sales counter, which are to be drawn on sheet P2-1 at 1/4" = 1'-0" (requirements follow).
4. Review all of the symbols and electrical requirements on sheet P2-2.
5. Locate the electrical and communication devices required on the electrical/data/phone plan, sheet P2-2.
6. Create a reflected ceiling plan on sheet P2-3 showing all lighting locations.
7. Draw required circuitry and switching locations for a functional design.
8. Write your control number where indicated in the lower right corner of every sheet—even the ones that you don't write on.
9. Select the best choice from the equipment listed in the legends and use only that equipment and those symbols. Do not add equipment or make up your own symbols.
10. Review P2-1 and note the location for elevations of the sales desk.

Code Requirements

- All electrical outlets must be located 18" AFF unless noted otherwise.
- Exit signage must be continuously visible along paths of travel toward exit to the outside.
- Where practical, wall outlets and ports are preferred over floor-mounted outlets and ports.
- Electricity, voice, and data devices required at the sales desk are to be brought up into and permanently affixed within the sales counter.

Additional Scope of Services

The coffee shop serves coffee and sandwiches and attracts customers for evening performances by musicians, poets, and performance artists. Coffee drinks are made to order at the service counter. A menu of made-to-order sandwiches and salads is displayed on the wall above the service counter. These orders are relayed electronically to the kitchen when the sale is rung up. Orders are delivered through a pass-through window from the kitchen to the service counter. Coffee is brewed and orders are assembled and wrapped at the back portion of the service counter.

Food items are packaged "to go" and may be carried away or eaten in the shop. Catering of sandwich-based meals is also available from the kitchen.

A small performance platform with flexible lighting serves a variety of small performances, including poetry and storytelling, musicians' performances, and performance art. An industrial atmosphere is requested.

Design Requirements

All items, adjacencies, and attributes mentioned in this document are required in your solution. Use a freehand sketch or drafting to represent items in accurate scale. Draw your solution on drawing sheets provided using ink or felt tip (it will be assumed that all pencil is preliminary to your final solution and not intended as part of your final solution).

Project Description

Service Counter—Front Counter
1. A computerized cash register sits on the sales counter at 36" AFF and is networked to a flat-panel display in the kitchen. The jack that connects and powers the register is to be located 24" AFF in a closed-door storage unit within the service counter, below the computer.
2. A phone is also located on the counter next to the register.
3. Drawer space for supplies to be aggregately (need not be a single drawer) 24" wide with a 6" tall drawer face and 10" deep with full-extension glides.
4. Indicate on the plan view with hidden lines and a note the barrier-free transaction surface at 30" high.
5. Two identical trash and paper refuse bins are each 14" × 18" × 31" tall.
6. Note materials to be used to create an industrial atmosphere.

The back service counter is not part of the design tasks for this exercise.

Electrical Plan
1. Review the requirements on sheet P2-2 and provide for all required devices.

Lighting/Reflected Ceiling Plan
1. Energy conservation to be balanced with effective lighting techniques in performance, dining, and sales areas.
2. Solution to be safe and conform with codes.

Timed Design
Exercise

Part 2 of 2

Floor Plan
Coffee Shop, Lite Version

Sheet   P2-1

Scale   1/8" = 1'-0"

Control Number

Performance
Platform

Kitchen

Accessible
Bathroom

Artwork Display Wall

Flat-Screen Display

Pass-
through

Front Service Counter

Sink

Use the space below to draw (to scale) your design for the service counter showing all
equipment devices, dimensions, and material descriptions.

(A) **Elevation of Customer Side of Service Counter**
Scale: 1/4" = 1'-0"

(B) **Elevation of Staff Side of Service Counter**
Scale: 1/4" = 1'-0"

Electrical/Data/Phone Plan
Coffee Shop, Lite Version

Sheet **P2-2**

Scale ⅛" = 1'-0"

Control Number

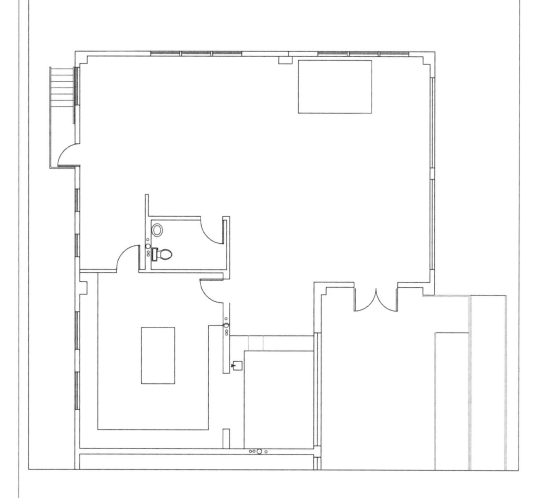

Electrical Legend

	Duplex outlet
GFI	Ground Fault Interrupt duplex outlet
	Quadruplex outlet
	220-volt outlet
	Cat 3 phone port
	Cat 5 data port
	Phone and data port
	Phone/data/power
	Floor duplex outlet
	Floor phone port
	Floor data port
H/D	Electric Hand Drier
	Recessed clock outlet for picture light

Use only these symbols to communicate your design. Do not make up your own symbols.

Equipment List
On your plan, note all heights that deviate from typical 18" AFF

Qty	Location and requirements
1	Service counter: phone/data/power in desktop
1	Service counter: 1 phone line 24" AFF
1	Duplex outlet in each side of performance platform
1	Phone/data/power 60" AFF for flat-panel display in kitchen
1	Duplex at 34" AFF cook's desk in kitchen
1	Voice/data/power 34" AFF cook's desk in kitchen
8	Convenience/duplex outlets for customers' laptop computers
1	Washroom one GFI outlet at sink in restroom 30" AFF
1	Electric hand drier in washroom

Refer to this list as you prepare your electrical/data/power plan; select and show only these items on that plan.

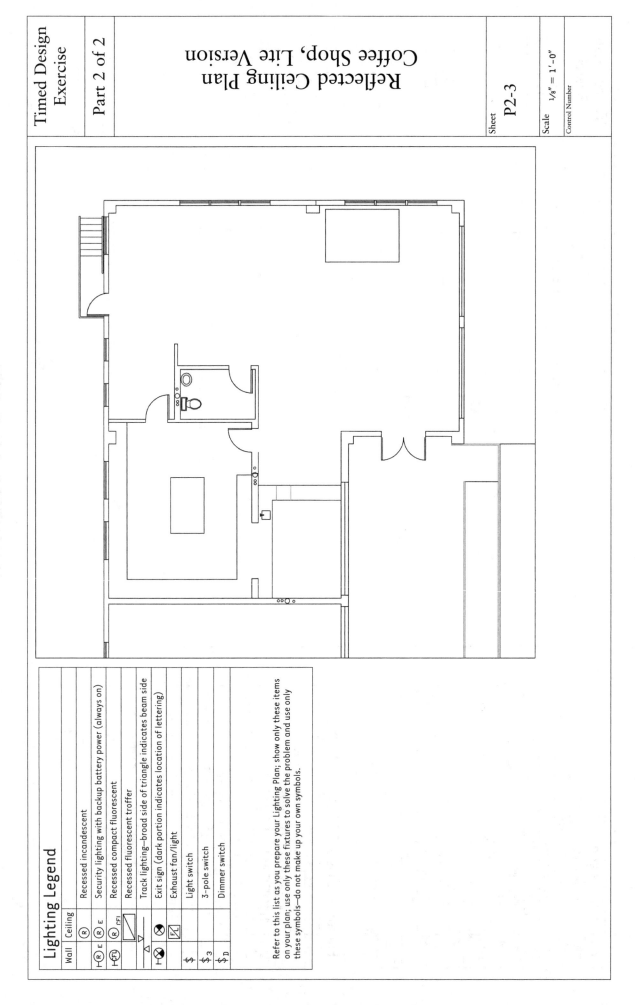

Timed Design Exercise

Part 2 of 2

Reflected Ceiling Plan
Coffee Shop, Lite Version

Sheet P2-3

Scale ⅛" = 1'-0"

Control Number

Lighting Legend

	Wall	Ceiling	
		®	Recessed incandescent
	⊢® E	® E	Security lighting with backup battery power (always on)
	⊢®F	®CF	Recessed compact fluorescent
		▱	Recessed fluorescent troffer
		▷	Track lighting—broad side of triangle indicates beam side
	⊢⊗	⊗	Exit sign (dark portion indicates location of lettering)
		FL	Exhaust fan/light
	⊄		Light switch
	⊄₃		3–pole switch
	⊄D		Dimmer switch

Refer to this list as you prepare your Lighting Plan; show only these items on your plan; use only these fixtures to solve the problem and use only these symbols—do not make up your own symbols.

DESIGN SCENARIO 3

Business Coach, Full Version

BUSINESS COACH

Full Version (141 points total)

Suggested Scoring Part One

The following *must* be met for 5 points each:

___ Living functions are not intermingled with studio functions except for theater conveniently located for use by both.

___ Paths of travel from office function do not have visual contact with living functions other than theater.

___ Safe egress is available to both functional spaces.

(15 points)

The following *must* be met for 2 points each:

___ Egress is not blocked, locked, or used for storage.

___ Paths of egress are barrier free and are a minimum of 44 inches wide.

___ The entrance, studio, and restroom are barrier free.

___ Doors along paths of exit travel are 36 inches wide and do not impinge upon clear 44-inch-wide path.

___ Open storage does not impinge on 44-inch-wide clear paths of exit travel.

___ Doors that are not along an exit path of travel are at least 30 inches clear open width.

___ Accessible doors (along egress routes for business function) have 18 inches clear wall space on the pull side of the latch edge and 12 inches on the pull side of the hinge edge.

___ Door swings do not encroach on turning circles.

___ Habitable spaces have natural light and ventilation.

___ Plumbing floor drain locations are within 8 feet of plumbing stacks raised drains (sinks and toilets NOTED as wall mounted) within 16 feet.

___ Pipes are concealed, not exposed, in solution.

___ Perimeter walls are centered on demark lines on given plan.

___ No window areas not given by scenario have been added and none are taken away.

___ Theater door into residence is discreetly positioned while door from theater to offices is grander/more emphasized.

___ Bathroom is adjacent to bedroom and separate from powder room, and both are separate from office powder room.

___ Bedroom has reasonable fire-escape access to window/room not furnished along entire window wall.

___ Solution is correctly portrayed entirely on sheet P1-2.

(34 points)

The following *must* to be evident on plan and matrix for 1 point each:

___ Adjacency matrix is complete and correct

___ Direct adjacency BRs to Bath

___ Direct adjacency Theater to Residence and Office

___ Direct adjacency Kitchen to Dining

___ Convenient adjacency Entrance to Living

___ Convenient adjacency Entertainment to Powder Room

___ Material schedule
Theater floor F-1 walls W-1
Bath floor F-3 walls W-3
Kitchen floor F-4 walls W-2
Office floor F-1 walls W-4

(7 points)

The following *should* be met for additional 1/2 point each (each requirement listed per space on C-1):

Office Area

Reception

___ Desk 72 inches × 30 inches

___ Return 24 inches × 72 inches

___ Two visitor chairs 10 feet or more from receptionist desk

___ Table surface reachable from each chair

Coaching Office

____ Four lounge chairs around a round coffee table

____ Desk 70 inches wide × 30 inches deep from front to back

____ Return 72 inches wide × 24 inches deep from front to back

Conference Rooms (Two)

____ Conference table for eight

____ Buffet 60 inches × 20 inches

____ Chairs 24 inches wide for formal atmosphere and comfort

Theater

____ Lounge seating for 10

____ Oriented to logical screen location

____ Logical equipment location for remote control and DVD access

Guest Powder Room

____ Toilet with grab bars noted

____ Accessible sink

Entrance

____ 75 inches × 24-inch-deep closet or 12 LF hook coat storage

____ 60 inches × 24 inches set-down surface with access to storage below

Living Room

____ Lounge seating for 10 with set-down surface at each seat

____ Game table for four convenient for use as dining table too

Dining Area

____ Table seating for 10

____ Buffet 72 feet long × 24 inches deep from front to back

Kitchen

____ 15 LF of base and 10 LF of uppers

____ Refrigerator 30 inches × 28 inches × 78 inches tall

____ Dishwasher 2 feet × 2 feet under counter shown with dotted line

____ Microwave 21 inches wide × 18 inches deep shown with dotted line if below counter

____ Sink 24 inches × 18 inches

Bedroom

____ Double bed approx 54 inches × 75 inches with minimum 2 feet clearance on each side

____ Nightstands 24 inches wide × 20 inches deep with clear space to access drawers below

____ Dresser 6 feet wide × 20 inches deep

____ Closet 16 feet LF of hanging

____ Desk 6 feet × 2½ feet

____ Closet with 4 feet of long hanging and 8 feet of short hanging

Bathroom

____ Vanity 30 inches wide × 22 inches deep from front to back; has one sink

____ Toilet

____ Tub with shower

____ Linen closet 2 feet × 2 feet

(18 points)

The following *should* be present for 1 point each:

____ No item of furniture taller than 3 feet should be placed in front of windows with 3-foot-high sill

____ All required items are illustrated or labeled to differentiate from other item types

____ Flow and logic prevail over choppy and cluttered layout

(3 points)

Suggested Scoring Part Two

The following *should* be met for 2 points each (overall quality issues):

____ Plans are completed using only the selections and symbols given

____ Outlets are noted at 18 inches AFF except for the sales desk outlets and devices

____ Exit signage positioned for visibility from all locations (except inside washroom)

____ Outlets are wall outlets wherever practical, including eight laptop outlet locations

(8 points)

Desk Elevations

The following *should* be met for 2 points each (each requirement listed for cabinetry):

___ Accurately sketched or drafted to scale as required by elevation markers

___ Projection screen indicated by dotted lines at crown on elevation

___ Four pieces of equipment indicated 17 inches wide × 13 inches deep × 6 inches tall

___ Left and right speakers 8 inches wide × 12 inches tall and 6 inches deep

___ Subwoofer concealed in cabinet sits on floor of room, not on floor of cabinet

___ Small refrigerator 24 inches wide × 34 inches tall × 24 inches deep concealed in closed cabinet

___ Materials are noted on elevation and section

___ Section shows equipment hookups and connection to power

___ Electrical for required equipment noted

___ Sufficient dimensions to comprehend design, locations for services, and storage and size of storage spaces

(20 points)

Electrical Plan (Each Requirement for Lighting and Electrical)

The following *should* be met for 1 point each:

Proofing Room

___ Two duplex outlets convenient to seating for laptops

___ Phone jack indicated for wall-mounted phone; height noted anywhere between 40 inches and 54 inches AFF

Media Cabinet in Proofing Room

___ Two voice/data/power 18 inches AFF may be noted at this location or as general note

___ One quad outlet for equipment height noted

___ One duplex indicated for projection screen height noted

___ RGB cable for equipment

Conference Room

___ Two floor-mounted duplex outlets for laptops

___ Phone jack for wall-mounted phone height noted (40 inches to 54 inches AFF)

___ Duplex noted at buffet with height between 30 inches and 42 inches AFF

Recording Room

___ Two power/data/phone at camera side of room

___ Two duplex outlets for laptops

___ One RGB cable at camera side of room

Washroom

___ GFI at sink

___ Hand drier

(14 points)

Lighting Plan

The following *must* be present for 2 points each:

___ Fluorescent lights for ambient light

___ Incandescent used only in accent and feature lighting

___ Exit signage visible from all locations in shop (outside of restroom)

___ Minimum four light fixtures in filming area

___ Minimum four light fixtures in conference room

___ Minimum four light fixtures in proofing room

___ Minimum one light fixture in each bathroom

___ One light fixture in hallway outside bathrooms

___ Exit signage

(18 points)

One point awarded for (common sense items not requested):

___ Fan/light in bathroom

___ Emergency lighting incorporated into scheme

___ Task lighting provided at media cabinet

___ Each incandescent lamp and foot of incandescent strip used multiplied by 2, and each fluorescent and exit light multiplied by 1 should not add up to more than 40

(4 points)

TIMED DESIGN EXERCISE

Instructions to Students

1. Read all of these instructions before beginning the exercise.
2. Review the project and code requirements as well as the site plan P1-1.
3. Review the matrix, material options, and material schedules on P1-1.
4. Review the interior elevation showing the window fenestration from the interior P1-1.
5. Review the floor plan P1-2.
6. Read the entire project description and carefully review the requirements in each area.
7. Complete the adjacency matrix P1-1.
8. Show your proposed layout on the sheet given to solve the problem defined (following).
9. Select finish materials for the floors and walls and indicate the best choice by circling it on the schedule P1-1.
10. Write your control number in the lower right of every sheet—even the ones that you don't write on.

Code Requirements

- Egress paths of travel may not pass through areas that may be blocked, locked, or used for storage.
- Barrier free requires a 5' turning circle (show as a dotted line) at every change in direction. Paths of travel not required for egress are not bound by this restriction.
- Egress must be provided from the residence without requiring the consultant to pass through the office to exit.
- Maintain a minimum width of 44" along accessible routes.
- Doors and storage units that open toward a path of travel may not limit the clear passage width when open.
- Doors to be a minimum of 3' clear width in all accessible spaces and a minimum 30" clear width otherwise.
- Doors in accessible areas must be flanked by clear wall space—18" on the pull side and 12" wide on the push side along the latching side.
- Sinks in barrier-free areas must have clear knee space below and may not encroach on the turning circle.
- Door swings may not encroach on turning circles.
- Habitable spaces in the living space/apartment must have an operable window.
- Floors in areas with sinks must be slip resistant.
- Surfaces in bathrooms and washrooms must be moisture resistant.

Design Requirements

All items, adjacencies, and attributes mentioned in this document are required in your passing solution. Use a freehand sketch or drafting to represent items in accurate scale. Draw your solution on drawing sheets provided using ink or felt tip (it will be assumed that all pencil is preliminary to your final solution and not intended as part of your final solution). You need only erase pencil marks that will interfere with comprehension of your solution.

Complete the partition and furniture plan on P1-1, showing typical required details (door swings, backs on chairs, pillows on bed, etc.) to the extent necessary to distinguish one type of item from another. Label all spaces listed in the project description. Include the lineal feet or cubic feet of storage required with the label for such items where the specific requirement is noted on the project requirements list.

Project Description

A business coach lives and works at this location in a large city. The building is a former light assembly plant and has been converted into mixed-use office and residential occupancy. The business and residence are to each have their own separate areas except they are to share a theater space. The theater is to be accoustically separated from both the residence and the business spaces but is to be accessible by both as well. Both the business and the residence are to have a formal atmosphere, and the residence may take on a professional atmosphere, as business clients are frequently entertained here.

Plumbing stacks flank support columns. Small circles indicate actual pipes that must be concealed in your solution to accommodate the request for a formal and successful atmosphere. Locate all floor drains within 8' of waste pipes. The exterior shell of the building cannot be changed. The limits of the client space are indicated by a single line. For the partition separating the client space from the corridor and office space, center a 6" thick wall directly on top of the single line, which indicates the limits of your client's space.

Requirements for each functional area follow. Address the items to be represented as well as adjacencies and privacy considerations. Functions may be combined as long as all requirements are met.

Office Area

The entire office area must be handicapped accessible, including the reception and office areas.

1. Reception area with a desk and return. The desk is to be 30" × 72" and the return is to be 24" × 72". Two visitor chairs located at least 10' from the receptionist (outside social distance) with a small table that can be easily reached from both chairs.
2. Small coaching office with 4 lounge chairs around a round coffee table and a desk 30" × 72" with a return of 24" × 72".
3. Two conference rooms with a large single table for 10 and a buffet surface with storage below.
4. Guest powder room with a toilet and sink. This room must be handicapped accessible.
5. Theater space to be accessible from the office as well as from the residence. Lounge seating for 10. This is to be a handicapped-accessible space. Discreetly position the door between the theater and the residence so business clients are not enticed to try to pass through it. Projector location noted on ceiling. 5 pieces of equipment 17" wide × 13" deep × 4" tall will be largely operated by remote control, but physical access to DVD player (one of the 5 pieces) is required.

Residence

Entry

1. Coat storage for 15 coats (5" per coat hanging in 2' deep closet or 12" wide on hooks)
2. Cabinet with set-down surface 24" deep × 60" wide with storage below.

Living/Entertaining Space

1. Lounge seating for 10 with convenient table surface attendant to each seat
2. Game table for 4 to be used for games as well as intimate dining.

Dining Area

1. Dining table to seat 10
2. Buffet surface 24" deep × 72" long

Kitchen

1. 15 lineal feet clear counter space over base cabinets and appliances
2. 10 lineal feet of upper cabinets
3. Full-height refrigerator 36" wide × 28" deep by 72" tall
4. Undercounter dishwasher 24" × 24"
5. Microwave 21" wide × 18" deep × 15" tall
6. Sink 24" wide × 18" deep from front to back

Sleep Space

1. Double bed 54" wide × 75" long
2. Pair of nightstands 24" wide × 20" deep × 26" tall, with drawer storage
3. Dresser 6' wide × 20" deep from front to back × 30" tall
4. Closet with 4' of long hanging and 8' of short/double hanging

Guest Powder Room

1. Toilet and sink
2. Storage for paper products

Bathroom

1. Vanity cabinet 30" wide × 22" deep containing sink
2. Toilet
3. Tub 2'-5" wide × 5'-0" long with shower. Indicate location of fittings (shower head and faucet)
4. Linen closet 24" wide × 24" deep full height

Timed Design Exercise

Part 1 of 2

Part One of Design Exercise
Business Coach, Full Version

Sheet

C-1

Scale   None

Student Control Number

Timed Design
Exercise

Part 1 of 2

Site Plan
Elevation
Matrix
Schedule
Business Coach, Full Version

Sheet

P1-1

Scale $\frac{1}{8}'' = 1'-0''$

Control Number

Design Scenario 3

Adjacency Matrix
Use only these symbols; do not make up your own symbols.

● Direct Adjacency
○ Convenient Adjacency
□ Visual Connection
X Remote

	Reception	Coaching	Conference	Restroom	Theater	Entry	Living/Ent.	Kitchen	Dining	Sleeping	Bath
Reception											
Coaching											
Conference											
Restroom											
Theater											
Entry											
Living/Ent.											
Kitchen											
Dining											
Sleeping											
Bath											

F	Floor
F1	45 oz level loop nylon carpet tiles
F2	Cut pile nylon carpet
F3	Marble tiles
F4	Stone-look porcelain tile
F5	Linoleum sheet goods
W	**Walls**
W1	Linen upholstered walls fire-rated
W2	Semigloss, low VOC paint
W3	Ceramic tile
W4	Textured commercial vinyl wall covering

Circle the most appropriate choice from those listed to the right by referencing the table above for material descriptions.

Area	Floor			Walls		
Theater	F1	F2	F5	W1	W3	W4
Bathroom	F2	F3	F5	W1	W2	W3
Kitchen	F1	F4	F5	W1	W3	W5
Office WC	F2	F3	F4	W1	W2	W4

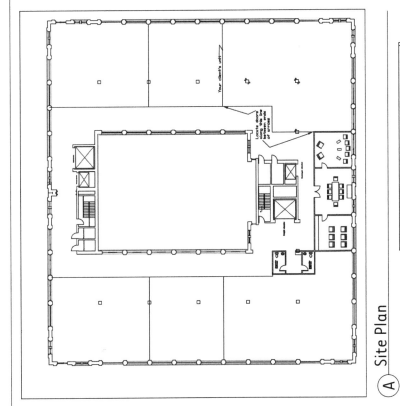

A Site Plan

B Interior Elevation
Scale ⅛" = 1'-0"

Business Coach, Full Version | **Timed Design Exercises** | Part 1 of 2 (CD)

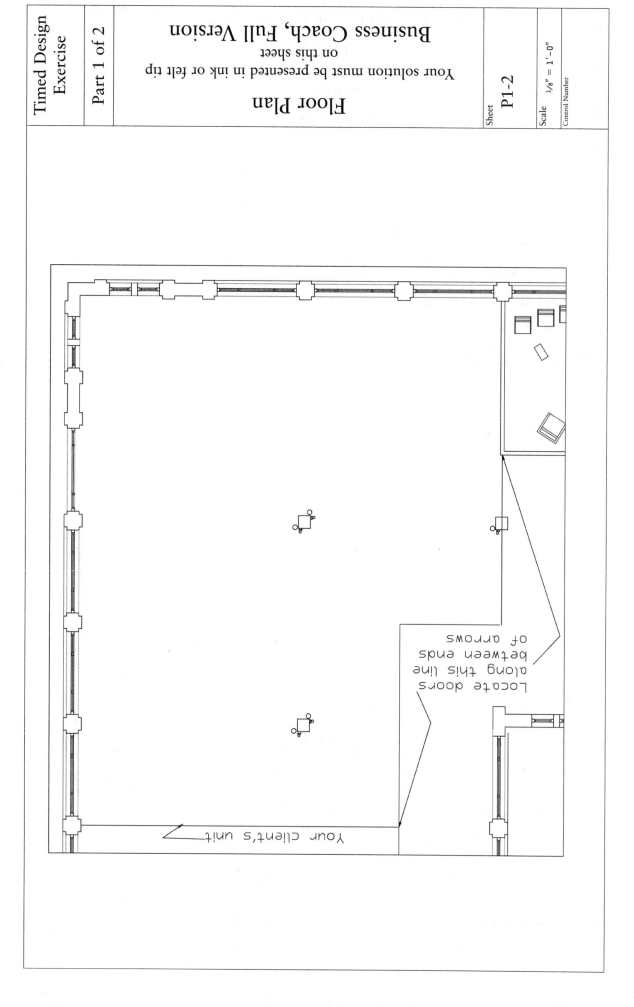

Timed Design
Exercise

Part 1 of 2

Business Coach, Full Version
on this sheet
Your solution must be presented in ink or felt tip

Floor Plan

Sheet P1-2

Scale ⅛" = 1'-0"

Control Number

Locate doors
along this line
between ends
of arrows

Your client's unit

TIMED DESIGN EXERCISE

Sheet

C-2

Scale   None

Student Control Number

Design Scenario 3

Instructions to Students

1. Read all of these instructions before beginning the exercise.
2. Review the project and code requirements and additional scope of services.
3. Review the floor plan P2-1; notice the layout for your lighting and electrical planning and also the elevation symbols indicating the elevation for the media cabinet, which is to be drawn on sheet P2-2 at 1/4" = 1'-0" (requirements follow). In addition to the elevation, draw a vertical section through the portion containing the 4 pieces of equipment showing how the design allows for the wiring between the equipment, TV, and speakers.
4. Review all of the symbols and electrical requirements on sheet P2-3.
5. Locate the electrical and communication devices required on the electrical/data/phone plan, sheet P2-3.
6. Create a reflected ceiling plan on sheet P2-4 showing all lighting locations.
7. Draw required circuitry and switching locations for a functional design.
8. Write your control number where indicated in the lower right corner of every sheet—even the ones that you don't write on.
9. Select the best choice from the equipment listed in the legends and use only that equipment and those symbols. Do not add equipment or make up your own symbols.

Code Requirements

● All electrical outlets must be located 18" AFF unless noted otherwise.
● Exit signage must be visible upon exiting all enclosed spaces and positioned to direct people safely out to the corridor.
● Where practical, wall outlets and ports are preferred over floor-mounted outlets and ports.
● Include in your solution exit signage in the hallway to continue to direct your client's visitors to the building's stairwell.
● Include in your solution exit signage required by code in your client's office suite.

Additional Scope of Services

Instructional audio and video presentations on CD and DVD are an important income stream for the coaching business. These discs are recorded in-house and edited by a consulting firm. Coaches in training are also filmed here. The proofing room is a second theater when needed and is also a convenient training space, as equipment here is connected to cameras in the recording space, and coaches in training can easily move back and forth between the two spaces. The conference room is frequently used for meetings and work sessions.

Design Requirements

All items, adjacencies, and attributes mentioned in this document are required in your solution. Use a freehand sketch or drafting to represent items in accurate scale. Draw your solution on drawing sheets provided using ink or felt tip (it will be assumed that all pencil is preliminary to your final solution and not intended as part of your final solution).

Project Description

Media Cabinet

1. The design of the media cabinet is to be congruent with a formal atmosphere.
2. A projection screen should be contained in the media cabinet, concealed in a crown detail integrated into the cabinet.
3. The cabinet is to also contain 4 pieces of sound equipment. Each is 17" wide × 13" deep × 4" tall.
4. Speakers are to be integrated into the cabinet. The left and right side channel and the center channel speakers are 8" wide × 12" tall × 6" deep.
5. The subwoofer is to sit directly on the floor inside the cabinet (the base may be cut out at that location). It is 15" square and 13" tall.
6. Cabinet is to house a small refrigerator that is 24" wide × 34" tall × 24" deep.
7. Label all finishes/surface materials for the desk; note incremental and overall dimensions.
8. Indicate location of electrical required to power the equipment contained in the cabinet with a hidden line if it falls behind equipment (solid line if it is visible when equipment is in place).
9. View Number One should show the cabinet as it would look with doors and speaker cloth removed to show equipment locations.
10. View Number Two should show the section through the equipment portion showing how the equipment connects to power and to other pieces of equipment when necessary.

Electrical Plan

1. Review the requirements on sheet P2-2 and provide for all required devices.

Lighting/Reflected Ceiling Plan

1. Energy conservation to be balanced with effective lighting techniques in display and sales areas.
2. Solution to be safe and conform with codes.

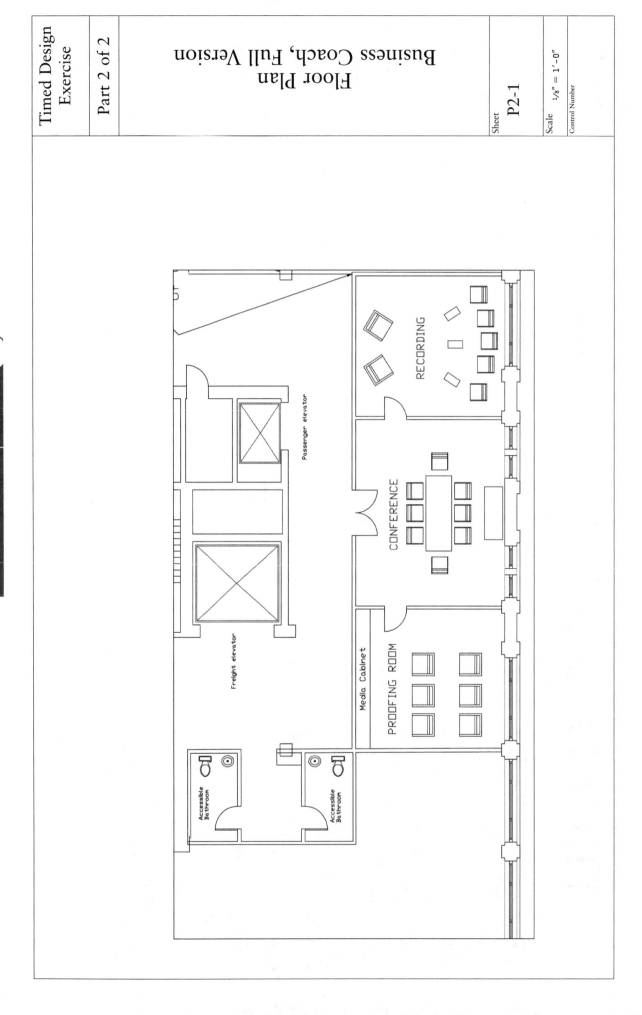

Timed Design
Exercise

Part 2 of 2

Floor Plan
Business Coach, Full Version

Sheet
P2-1

Scale   1/8" = 1'-0"

Control Number

Electrical/Data/Phone Plan
Business Coach, Full Version

Sheet

P2-2

Scale: 1/8" = 1'-0"

Control Number

Use the space below to draw (to scale) your design for the media cabinet showing all equipment devices, dimensions, and material descriptions.

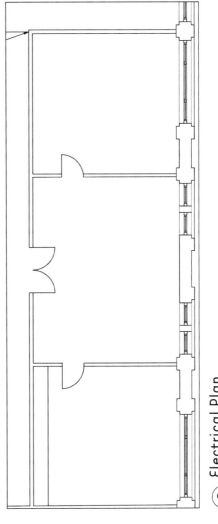

B Section Through Media Cabinet
Scale: 1/4" = 1'-0"

A Elevation of Media Cabinet
Scale: 1/4" = 1'-0"

C Electrical Plan
Scale: 1/8" = 1'-0"

Electrical Legend

⊕	Duplex outlet
⊕GFI	Ground Fault Interrupt duplex outlet
⊕	Quadruplex outlet
⊕	220-volt outlet
▽	Cat 3 phone port
▽VID	Shielded RGB video port
▼	Phone and data port
⊕	Phone/data/power
▣	Floor duplex outlet
▽	Floor phone port
▼	Floor data port

Use only these symbols to communicate your design. Do not make up your own symbols.

Equipment List
Note on your plan heights for all locations deviating from typical of 18" AFF

Qty	Location and requirements
2	Media cabinet: phone/data/power
1	Media cabinet: one quadruplex outlet for equipment
1	Media cabinet: duplex at projection screen location
2	Proofing room convenience outlets for laptops
1	Proofing room phone jack for wall-mounted phone
1	Media cabinet RGB video port
1	Conference room: phone jack for wall-mounted phone
2	Conference table: duplex floor outlets for laptops
1	Conference buffet to conceal duplex convenient to its top
2	Recording room: power/data/phone port for cameras
2	Recording room: duplex convenience outlet
4	Recording room: ports for RGB video cable one ea. camera

Refer to this list as you prepare your electrical/data/power plan; select and show only these items on that plan.

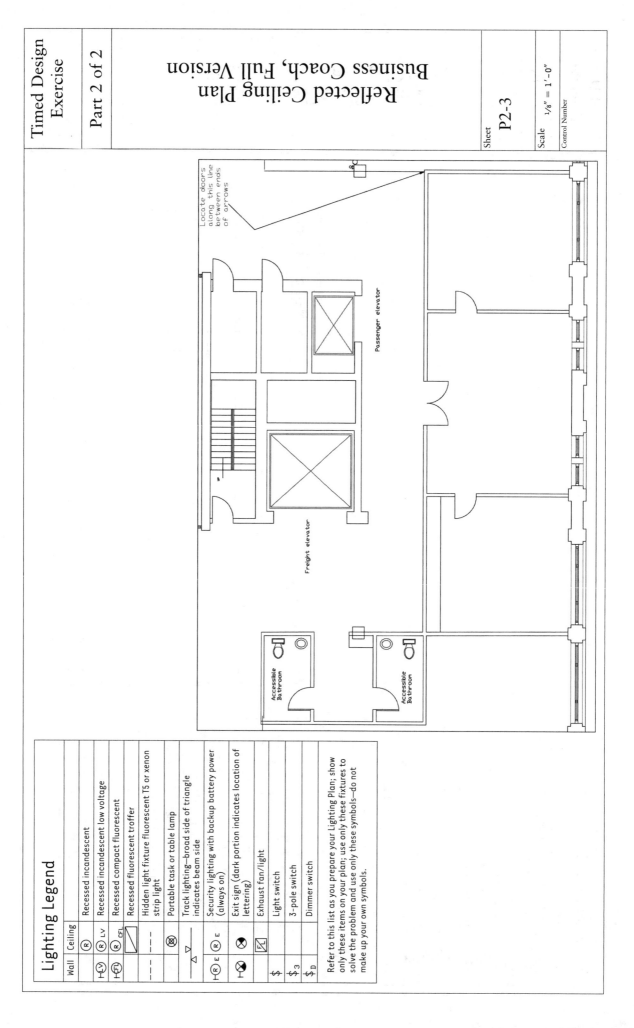

Timed Design Exercise

Part 2 of 2

Reflected Ceiling Plan
Business Coach, Full Version

Sheet P2-3

Scale ⅛" = 1'-0"

Control Number

Lighting Legend

Wall	Ceiling	
	ℝ	Recessed incandescent
	ℝ LV	Recessed incandescent low voltage
	ℝ CF	Recessed compact fluorescent
		Recessed fluorescent troffer
		Hidden light fixture fluorescent T5 or xenon strip light
	⊗	Portable task or table lamp
	▽	Track lighting—broad side of triangle indicates beam side
ℝ E	ℝ E	Security lighting with backup battery power (always on)
⊗	⊗	Exit sign (dark portion indicates location of lettering)
	FL	Exhaust fan/light
$		Light switch
$3		3-pole switch
$D		Dimmer switch

Refer to this list as you prepare your Lighting Plan; show only these items on your plan; use only these fixtures to solve the problem and use only these symbols—do not make up your own symbols.

Locate doors along this line between ends of arrows

Passenger elevator

Freight elevator

Accessible Bathroom

Accessible Bathroom

DESIGN SCENARIO 3

Business Coach, Lite Version

BUSINESS COACH

Lite Version (122 points total)

Suggested Scoring Part One

The following *must* be met for 5 points:

___ Living functions are not intermingled with studio functions except for the theater conveniently located for use by both.

___ Paths of travel from office function do not have visual contact with living functions other than theater.

___ Safe egress is available to both functional spaces.
(15 points)

The following *must* be met for 2 points each (code requirements listed on C-1 and info on P1-1):

___ Egress is not blocked, locked, or used for storage.

___ Paths of egress are barrier free and are a minimum of 44 inches wide.

___ The entrance, studio, and restroom are barrier free.

___ Doors along paths of exit travel are 36 inches wide and do not impinge upon clear 44-inch-wide path.

___ Open storage does not impinge on 44 inch-wide clear paths of exit travel.

___ Doors that are not along an exit path of travel are at least 30 inches clear open width.

___ Accessible doors (along egress routes for business function) have 18 inches clear wall space on the pull side of the latch edge and 12 inches on the pull side of the hinge edge.

___ Door swings do not encroach on turning circles.

___ Habitable spaces have natural light and ventilation.

___ Plumbing floor drain locations are within 8 feet of plumbing stacks raised drains (sinks and toilets NOTED as wall mounted) within 16 feet.

___ Pipes are concealed, not exposed, in solution.

___ Living and business functions are not intermingled.

___ No window areas not given by scenario have been added and none are taken away.

___ Theater door into residence is discreetly positioned, while door from theater to offices is grander.

___ Bedroom has reasonable fire-escape access to window/room not furnished along entire window wall.

___ Solution is correctly portrayed entirely on sheet P1-2.
(32 points)

The following *should* be correctly shown on matrix and plan for 1 point each:

___ Direct adjacency BRs to Bath

___ Direct adjacency Kitchen to Dining

___ Convenient adjacency Entrance to Living

___ Convenient adjacency Entertainment to Powder Room

___ Material schedule
Reception floor F-1 walls W-1
Bath floor F-3 walls W-3
Kitchen floor F-4 walls W-2
Bedroom floor F-2 walls W-1
(5 points)

The following *should* be met for a ¹/₂ point each:

Office Area

Reception

___ Desk 72 inches × 30 inches

___ Return 24 inches × 72 inches

___ Two visitor chairs 10 feet or more from receptionist desk

___ Table surface reachable from each chair

Coaching Office

___ Four lounge chairs around a round coffee table

___ Desk 70 inches wide × 30 inches deep from front to back

___ Return 72 inches wide × 24 inches deep from front to back

Conference Room

____ Conference table for 10

____ Buffet 60 inches × 20 inches

____ Chairs 24 inches wide for formal atmosphere and comfort

Guest Powder Room

____ Toilet with grab bars noted

____ Accessible sink

____ Accessible to business and residence without excessive travel into space to reach

Living Area

Entrance

____ 75 inches × 24-inch-deep closet or 12 LF hook coat storage

____ 60 inches × 24 inches set-down surface with access to storage below

Living Room

____ Lounge seating for eight

____ Set-down surface at each seat

____ Game table for four convenient for use as dining table too

____ Flatscreen TV above equipment cabinet that is 5 feet × 2 feet

____ TV comfortably viewable from four lounge seats

Dining Area

____ Table seating for eight

____ Buffet 72 feet long × 24 inches deep from front to back

Kitchen

____ 15 LF of base

____ 10 LF of uppers

____ Refrigerator 30 inches × 28 inches × 78 inches tall

____ Dishwasher 2 feet × 2 feet under counter shown with dotted line

____ Microwave 21 inches wide x 18 inches deep shown with dotted line if below counter

____ Sink 24 inches × 18 inches

____ Range 30 inches wide × 28 inches deep from front to back

Bedroom

____ Double bed approx 54 inches × 75 inches with minimum 2 feet clearance on each side

____ Nightstands 24 inches wide × 20 inches deep with clear space to access drawers below

____ Dresser 6 feet wide × 20 inches deep

____ Closet with 3 feet of long hanging and 4 feet of short hanging

Bathroom

____ Vanity 30 inches wide × 22 inches deep from front to back has one sink

____ Toilet

____ Tub with shower

____ Linen closet 2 feet × 2 feet

____ No item of furniture taller than 3 feet should be placed in front of windows with 3-foot-high sill

____ All required items are illustrated or labeled to differentiate from other item types

____ Flow and logic prevail over choppy and cluttered layout

(20 points)

Suggested Scoring Part Two

The following *should* be met for 2 points each:

____ Plans are completed using only the selections and symbols given

____ Outlets are noted at 18 inches AFF except for the sales desk outlets and devices

____ Exit signage positioned for visibility from all locations (except inside washroom)

____ Outlets are wall outlets wherever practical, including eight laptop outlet locations

(8 points)

Desk Elevations

The following *should* be met for 2 points each:

____ The desk is accurately sketched or drafted to scale as required by elevation markers

____ Appearance congruent with formal atmosphere

____ Location shown for four pieces of equipment 17 inches × 13 inches × 4 inches tall

____ Left and right speakers 8 inches wide × 12 inches tall

____ Materials are noted on both interior and exterior views

(10 points)

Electrical Plan

The following *should* be met for 1 point each:

Proofing Room

___ Duplex convenience outlet at location convenient to seating

___ Phone jack for wall-mounted phone height noted between 40 inches and 54 inches AFF

___ Duplex outlet in ceiling above media cabinet for projection screen

Media Cabinet in Proofing Room

___ Two voice/data/power

___ Quad outlet for equipment in cabinet

___ One RGB video cable

Conference Room

___ Phone jack for wall-mounted phone height noted between 40 inches and 54 inches AFF

___ Two floor-mounted duplex outlets under table

Filming Room

___ Two voice/data/power at camera end

___ Four RGB ports at camera side of room

(10 points)

Lighting Plan

The following *must* be met for 2 points each:

___ Fluorescent lights for ambient light

___ Incandescent used only in accent and feature lighting

___ Exit signage visible from all locations in shop (outside of restroom)

___ Minimum four light fixtures in filming area

___ Minimum four light fixtures in conference room

___ Minimum four light fixtures in proofing room

___ Minimum one light fixture in each bathroom

___ One light fixture in hallway outside bathrooms

___ Exit signage

(18 points)

The following *should* be met for 1 point each:

___ Fan/light in bathroom

___ Emergency lighting incorporated into scheme

___ Task lighting provided at media cabinet

___ Each incandescent lamp and foot of incandescent strip used multiplied by 2, plus each fluorescent and exit light multiplied by 1, should not add up to more than 30

(4 points)

TIMED DESIGN EXERCISE

Part One of Design Exercise
Business Coach, Lite Version

Timed Design Exercise

Part 1 of 2

Sheet C-1

Scale None

Student Control Number

Instructions to Students

1. Read all of these instructions before beginning the exercise.
2. Review the project and code requirements as well as the site plan P1-1.
3. Review the matrix, material options, and material schedules on P1-1.
4. Review the interior elevation showing the window fenestration from the interior P1-1.
5. Review the floor plan P1-2.
6. Read the entire project description and carefully review the requirements in each area.
7. Complete the adjacency matrix P1-1.
8. Show your proposed layout on the sheet given to solve the problem defined (following).
9. Select finish materials for the floors and walls and indicate the best choice by circling it on the schedule P1-1.
10. Write your control number in the lower right of every sheet—even the ones that you don't write on.

Code Requirements

- Egress paths of travel may not pass through areas that may be blocked, locked, or used for storage.
- Barrier free requires a 5' turning circle (show as a dotted line) at every change in direction. Paths of travel not required for egress are not bound by this restriction.
- Egress must be provided from the residence without requiring the consultant to pass through the office to exit.
- Maintain a minimum width of 44" along accessible routes.
- Doors and storage units that open toward a path of travel may not limit the clear passage width when open.
- Doors to be a minimum of 3' clear width in all accessible spaces and a minimum 30" clear width otherwise.
- Doors in accessible areas must be flanked by clear wall space—18" on the pull side and 12" wide on the push side along the latching side.
- Sinks in barrier-free areas must have clear knee space below and may not encroach on the turning circle more than 6".
- Door swings may not encroach on turning circles.
- Habitable spaces in the living space/apartment must have an operable window.
- Floors in areas with sinks must be slip resistant.
- Surfaces in bathrooms and washrooms must be moisture resistant.

Design Requirements

All items, adjacencies, and attributes mentioned in this document are required in your passing solution. Use a freehand sketch or drafting to represent items in accurate scale. Draw your solution on drawing sheets provided using ink or felt tip (it will be assumed that all pencil is preliminary to your final solution and not intended as part of your final solution). You need only erase pencil marks that will interfere with comprehension of your solution.

Complete the partition and furniture plan on P1-1, showing typical required details (door swings, backs on chairs, pillows on bed, etc.) to the extent necessary to distinguish one type of item from another. Label all spaces listed in the project description. Include the lineal feet or cubic feet of storage required with the label for such items where the specific requirement is noted on the project requirements list.

Project Description

A business coach lives and works at this location in a large city. The building is a former light assembly plant and has been converted into mixed-use office and residential occupancy. The business and residence are to each have their own separate areas except they are to share an entrance hallway and a powder room (must be barrier free). Both business and the residence are to have a formal atmosphere, and the residence may take on a professional atmosphere, as business clients are frequently entertained here.

Plumbing stacks flank support columns. Small circles indicate actual pipes that must be concealed in your solution to accommodate the request for a formal and successful atmosphere. Locate all floor drains within 12' of waste pipes. The exterior shell of the building cannot be changed. The limits of the client space are indicated by a single line. For the partition separating the client space from the corridor and office space, center a 6" thick wall directly on top of the single line, which indicates the limits of your client's space.

Requirements for each functional area follow. Address the items to be represented as well as adjacencies and privacy considerations. Functions may be combined as long as all requirements are met.

Office Area

The entire office area must be handicapped accessible, including the reception and office areas.

1. Reception area with a desk and return. The desk is to be 30" × 72" and the return is to be 24" × 72". Two visitor chairs located at least 10' from the receptionist (outside social distance) with a small table that can be easily reached from both chairs.
2. Small coaching office with 4 lounge chairs around a round coffee table and a desk 30" × 72" with a return of 24" × 72".
3. Conference room with a large single table for 10 and a buffet surface with storage below.

Residence

Entry
1. Coat storage for 15 coats (5" per coat hanging in 2' deep closet or 12" wide on hooks)
2. Cabinet with set-down surface 24" deep × 60" wide with storage below.

Living/Entertaining Space
1. Lounge seating for 8 with convenient table surface attendant to each seat
2. Game table for 4
3. Flat-screen TV above a console for equipment. Console to be 2' deep from front to back × 5' wide. This TV must be comfortably viewable from at least 4 of the chairs.

Dining Area
1. Dining table to seat 8
2. Buffet surface 24" deep × 72" long

Kitchen
1. 15 lineal feet clear counter space over base cabinets and appliances
2. 10 lineal feet of upper cabinets
3. Full-height refrigerator 36" wide × 28" deep by 72" tall
4. Undercounter dishwasher 24" × 24"
5. Microwave 21" wide × 18" deep × 15" tall
6. Sink 24" wide × 18" deep from front to back
7. Range 30" wide × 24" deep from front to back

Sleep Space
1. Double bed 54" wide × 75" long
2. Pair of nightstands 24" wide × 20" deep × 26" tall, with drawer storage
3. Dresser 6' wide × 20" deep from front to back × 30" tall
4. Closet with 3' of long hanging and 4' of short/double hanging

Guest Powder Room
1. Toilet and sink
2. Storage for paper products

Bathroom
1. Vanity cabinet 30" wide × 22" deep containing sink
2. Toilet
3. Tub 2'-5" wide × 5'-0" long with shower. Indicate location of fittings (shower head and faucet)
4. Linen closet 24" wide × 24" deep full height

Site Plan
Elevation
Matrix
Schedule
Business Coach, Lite Version

Sheet **P1-1**

Scale As Noted

Control Number

Adjacency Matrix

Use only these symbols; do not make up your own symbols.

● Direct Adjacency
○ Convenient Adjacency
□ Visual Connection
X Remote

	Reception	Coaching	Conference	Powder Rm	Entry	Living/Ent.	Kitchen	Dining	Sleeping	Bath
Reception										
Coaching										
Conference										
Powder Rm										
Entry										
Living/Ent.										
Kitchen										
Dining										
Sleeping										
Bath										

F	Floor
F1	45 oz level loop nylon carpet
F2	Cut pile nylon carpet
F3	Marble tiles
F4	Stone look porcelain tile
F5	Linoleum sheet goods
W	Walls
W1	Linen upholstered walls fire-rated
W2	Semigloss, low VOC paint
W3	Ceramic tile
W4	Textured commercial vinyl wall covering

Circle the most appropriate choice from those listed to the right by referencing the table above for material descriptions.

Area	Floor			Walls		
Reception	F1	F2	F5	W1	W3	W4
Bathroom	F2	F3	F5	W1	W2	W3
Kitchen	F1	F3	F5	W1	W2	W4
Bedroom	F2	F3	F4	W1	W3	W4

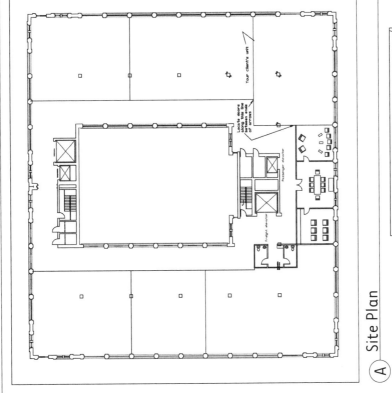

A Site Plan

B Interior Elevation
Scale 1/8" = 1'-0"

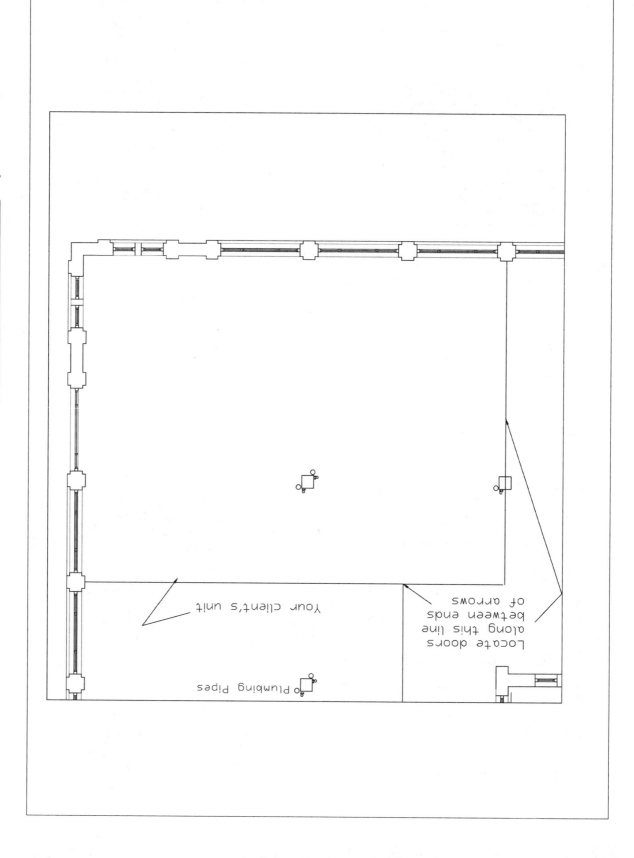

Timed Design Exercise
Part 1 of 2

Business Coach, Lite Version

Your solution must be presented in ink or felt tip on this sheet

Floor Plan

Sheet **P1-2**

Scale ⅛" = 1'-0"

Control Number

Your client's unit

Plumbing Pipes

Locate doors along this line between ends of arrows

Timed Design Exercise

Part 2 of 2

Part Two of Design Exercise
Business Coach, Lite Version

Sheet

C-2

Scale   None

Student Control Number

117

Design Scenario 3

TIMED DESIGN EXERCISE

Instructions to Students

1. Read all of these instructions before beginning the exercise.
2. Review the project and code requirements and additional scope of services.
3. Review the floor plan P2-1, notice the layout for your lighting and electrical planning and also the elevation symbols indicating the vantage point for the two elevations required for the media cabinet, which is to be drawn on sheet P2-1 at 1/4" = 1'-0" (requirements follow).
4. Review all of the symbols and electrical requirements on sheet P2-3.
5. Locate the electrical and communication devices required on the electrical/data/phone plan sheet P2-3.
6. Create a reflected ceiling plan on sheet P2-4 showing all lighting locations.
7. Draw required circuitry and switching locations for a functional design.
8. Write your control number where indicated in the lower right corner of every sheet—even the ones that you don't write on.
9. Select the best choice from the equipment listed in the legends and use only that equipment and those symbols. Do not add equipment or make up you own symbols.

Code Requirements

- All electrical outlets must be located 18" AFF unless noted otherwise.
- Exit signage must be visible upon exiting all enclosed spaces and positioned to direct people out safely to the corridor.
- Where practical, wall outlets and ports are preferred over floor-mounted outlets and ports.
- Include in your solution exit signage in the hallway to continue to direct your client's visitors to the building's stairwell.
- Include in your solution exit signage required by code in your client's office suite.

Additional Scope of Services

Instructional audio and video presentations on CD and DVD are an important income stream for the coaching business. These discs are recorded in-house and edited by a consulting firm. Coaches in training are also filmed here. The proofing room is a theater when needed and a convenient training space, as equipment here is connected to cameras in the recording space, and coaches in training can easily move back and forth between the two spaces. The conference room is frequently used for meetings and work sessions.

Design Requirements

All items, adjacencies, and attributes mentioned in this document are required in your solution. Use a freehand sketch or drafting to represent items in accurate scale. Draw your solution on drawing sheets provided using ink or felt tip (it will be assumed that all pencil is preliminary to your final solution and not intended as part of your final solution).

Project Description

Media Cabinet

1. The design of the media cabinet is to be congruent with a formal atmosphere.
2. The cabinet is to also contain 4 pieces of sound equipment. Each is 17" wide × 13" deep × 4" tall.
3. Speakers are to be integrated into the cabinet. The left and right side channel and the center channel speakers are 8" wide × 12" tall × 6" deep. Label all finishes/surface materials for the desk, note incremental and overall dimensions.
5. View Number One should show the cabinet as it would look with doors and speaker cloth removed to show equipment locations.
6. View Number Two should show the appearance of the cabinet with doors and speaker cloth in place.

Electrical Plan

1. Review the requirements on sheet P2-2 and provide for all required devices.

Lighting/Reflected Ceiling Plan

1. Energy conservation to be balanced with effective lighting techniques in display and sales areas.
2. Solution to be safe and conform with codes.

Timed Design
Exercise

Part 2 of 2

Floor Plan
Business Coach, Lite Version

Sheet

P2-1

Scale   1/8" = 1'-0"

Control Number

Use the space below to draw (to scale) your design for the media cabinet showing
all equipment devices, dimensions, and material descriptions.

A   Elevation of Media Cabinet Storage Exposed
Scale: 1/4" = 1'-0"

B   Elevation of Media Cabinet Appearance When Closed
Scale: 1/4" = 1'-0"

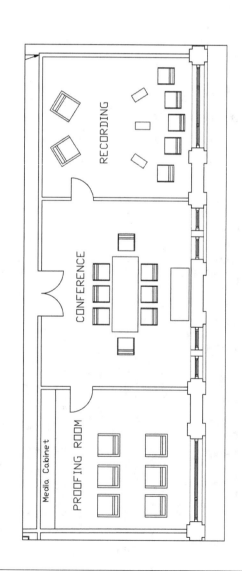

Media Cabinet

PROOFING ROOM

CONFERENCE

RECORDING

Electrical/Data/Phone Plan
Business Coach, Lite Version

Electrical Legend

	Duplex outlet
GFI	Ground Fault Interrupt duplex outlet
	Quadruplex outlet
	220-volt outlet
	Cat 3 phone port
	Shielded RGB video port
	Phone and data port
	Phone/data/power
	Floor duplex outlet
	Floor phone port
	Floor data port

Use only these symbols to communicate your design.. Do not make up your own symbols.

Equipment List Note on your plan heights for all locations deviating from typical of 18" AFF

Qty	Location and requirements
2	Media cabinet: phone/data/power
1	Media cabinet: one quadruplex outlet for equipment
1	Media cabinet: duplex in ceiling for projection screen
2	Proofing room convenience outlets for laptops
1	Proofing room phone jack for wall-mounted phone
1	Media cabinet RGB video port for communication with equipt.
1	Conference room: phone jack for wall-mounted phone
2	Conference table: duplex floor outlets for laptops
2	Recording room: power/data/phone port for cameras
4	Recording room: ports for RGB video cable one ea. camera

Refer to this list as you prepare your electrical/data/power plan; select and show only these items on that plan.

A Electrical Plan
Scale: 1/8" = 1'-0"

Timed Design Exercise
Part 2 of 2

Reflected Ceiling Plan
Business Coach, Lite Version

Sheet **P2-3**

Scale 1/8" = 1'-0"

Control Number

Lighting Legend

Wall	Ceiling	
	Ⓡ	Recessed incandescent
Ⓡ—Ⓛⱽ	Ⓡ ʟᵥ	Recessed incandescent low voltage
Ⓡ—Ⓕ	Ⓡ CFL	Recessed compact fluorescent
	▨	Recessed fluorescent troffer
– – –	– – –	Hidden light fixture fluorescent T5 or xenon strip light
✳	✳	Exit sign (dark portion indicates location of lettering)
▷	▷—	Track lighting—broad side of triangle indicates beam side
$		Light switch
$₃		3–pole switch
$ᴅ		Dimmer switch

Refer to this list as you prepare your Lighting Plan; show only these items on your plan; use only these fixtures to solve the problem and use only these symbols—do not make up your own symbols.

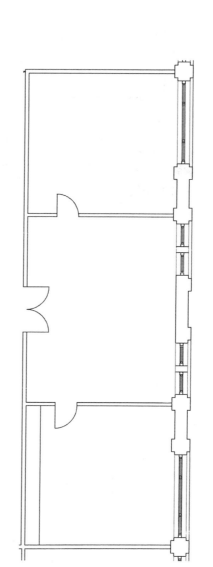

DESIGN SCENARIO 4

River Keeper's Station,
Full Version

RIVER KEEPER'S STATION

Full Version (132 points total)

Suggested Scoring Part One

The following *must* be met for 5 points:

___ Living functions are not intermingled with business functions.

___ Private living areas are to be visually screened.

___ Safe egress is available to both functional spaces.

(15 points)

The following *must* be met for 2 points each:

___ Egress is not blocked, locked, or used for storage.

___ Paths of egress are barrier free and a minimum of 44 inches wide.

___ Facility to be barrier free with the exception of three sleeping and bath spaces.

___ One BR/bath must be barrier free.

___ Safe and quick egress provided from sleeping areas.

___ Doors along paths of exit travel are 36 inches wide and do not impinge upon clear 44-inch-wide path.

___ Open storage does not impinge on 44-inch-wide clear paths of exit travel.

___ Doors that are not along an exit path of travel nor in handicapped-accessible areas are at least 30 inches clear open width.

___ Accessible doors have 18 inches clear wall space on the pull side of the latch edge and 12 inches on the pull side of the hinge edge with a clear width of 32 inches.

___ Door swings do not encroach on turning circles.

___ Habitable spaces have natural light and ventilation.

___ Access to business functions can be gained without extensive travel through living space.

___ All drains fall within a 36-foot-diameter circle, which is shown on the plan as a dotted line.

___ Windows and doors are shown correctly.

___ Consideration of rhythm of fenestration is evident in window placement.

___ Solution is correctly portrayed entirely on sheet P1-2.

___ Configuration and furnishings located to maximize views.

(34 points)

The following *should* be demonstrated on matrix and plan for 1 point:

___ Direct adjacency BRs to Baths

___ Direct adjacency Powder Room to Meeting Room

___ Direct adjacency Kitchen to Dining

___ Convenient adjacency Entrance to Living Room

___ Convenient adjacency Living Room to Powder Room

___ Convenient adjacency Entrance to Meeting Room

___ Material schedule
Classroom floor F-4 walls W-4
Lab floor F-2 walls W-1
Guest BR floor F-1 walls W-4
Kitchen floor F-4 walls W-1

(7 points)

The following *should* be met for additional ½ point each (each requirement listed per space on C-1):

Lab

___ Desk with 12 SF of surface with chair

___ Sink 30 inches wide × 20 inches deep from front to back noted for chemicals only (no plumbing)

___ Cabinet 30 inches wide × 18 inches deep noted locked for chemicals

___ Two stations each having:
12 LF counter 30 inches deep
Sink 12 inches × 18 inches
Storage below counter accessible

Research and Records

___ Two desks with 12 SF of surface and two executive chairs

___ 24 feet of lateral files

___ 25 linear feet of book shelves

___ Lounge chair and ottoman

___ Set-down surface and floor-standing task lamp at lounge chair

River Supplies

___ Closet 4 feet wide and 2 feet deep with hang rod

___ Bench 5 feet x 1½ feet form to back

___ Locked cabinet for keys 10 inches tall, 10 inches wide, 4 inches deep

___ Mounting height for above cabinet noted in range convenient for standing adult

___ Drip tray with drain 2 feet × 2 feet with hang rod

___ Door located on river side of this room

Utility Room

___ 120 SF shown within plumbing circle

Classroom

___ 20 chairs with flip-up writing surface

___ Folding table for presenter 30 inches × 60 inches with three chairs

___ Projector indicated with dotted line

___ Projection screen indicated with dotted line, 5 feet wide

___ Closet 30 inches deep from front to back and 5 feet wide

___ Barrier free

Living Room

___ Lounge seating for six

___ Set-down surface at each seat

___ Shelving unit for TV and stereo minimum 30 inches wide × 24 inches deep from front to back

___ 40 LF of book shelves

Kitchen

___ 15 LF of base and 10 LF of uppers

___ Refrigerator 30 inches × 28 inches × 72 inches tall

___ Dishwasher 2 feet × 2 feet

___ Microwave 21 inches wide × 18 inches deep

___ Sink 24 inches × 18 inches

___ Range 24 inches wide × 30 inches deep

___ Table and seating for six

Grad Student Sleep Spaces

___ Two such spaces

___ Double bed (54 inches × 75 inches) with minimum 2 feet clearance on each side

___ Set-down surface on each side, minimum 24 inches wide × 20 inches deep

___ Dresser 6 feet wide × 20 inches deep

___ Closet 3 LF of long hanging and 4 LF of short hanging

Visitors' Bedrooms

___ Two such spaces

___ Double bed with 2-foot clearance minimum on three sides

___ Pair of nightstands with drawer storage

___ Closet 1½ feet of hanging rod

___ Luggage stand 2 feet wide × ⅕ inches deep from front to back

___ One room to be barrier free

Grad Private Baths

___ Vanity 30 inches wide × 22 inches deep with one sink

___ Toilet and tub (2½ feet × 5 feet)

___ Linen closet 2 feet × 2 feet full height

Guest Bath

___ One bath shared by two visitors

___ Toilet

___ Shower minimum 3 feet × 3 feet

___ Located to function as powder room

___ Barrier free

One point awarded for each of the following:

___ All required items are illustrated or labeled to differentiate from other item types

___ Flow and logic prevail over choppy and cluttered layout

(27 points)

Suggested Scoring Part Two

The following *should* be met for 2 points each (overall quality issues):

___ Plans are completed using only the selections and symbols given

___ Outlets are noted at 18 inches AFF Floor Typ. except where instructed otherwise

___ Exit signage positioned for visibility from all locations (except inside washroom)

___ Outlets are wall outlets wherever practical

(8 points)

Reception Desk Elevations

The following *should* be met for 2 points each:

___ The desk is accurately sketched or drafted to scale as required by elevation markers

___ Materials noted congruent with nature themes

___ 30-inch desk height at computer

___ Phone jack in vertical support for transaction surface

___ Printer on pull out shelf below desktop

___ Two trash containers 8 inches × 12 inches × 15 inches tall

___ Box/file pedestal

___ Closed storage for paper

___ Dotted lines show locations of required elements not shown by views assigned

(18 points)

Electrical Plan (Each Requirement for Lighting and Electrical)

The following *should* be met for 1 point each:

Reception Desk

___ Voice/data/power

___ Phone

___ Duplex 24 inches AFF

Conference Room

___ Voice /Data/Power under conference table

___ Duplex at credenza

Warden Desk

___ Voice/data/power in wall convenient to desk

___ Duplex in wall convenient to desk

___ Phone jack in wall convenient to desk

___ Duplex in floor under community meeting table

___ Duplex in closet for DustBuster

___ Recessed clock outlet

(11 points)

Lighting Plan

The following *should* be met for 1 point each:

___ Fluorescent lights for ambient light

___ Flexible track for performance lighting

___ Exit signage visible from all locations in shop (outside of restroom)

___ Minimum two light fixtures in conference room

___ Minimum five light fixtures in reception/community table room

___ Minimum two light fixtures in each office

___ Minimum one light fixture in washroom

___ Minimum one light fixture in locked storage

(8 points)

The following *should* be met for 1 point each:

___ Fan/light in bathroom

___ Emergency lighting incorporated into scheme

___ Task lighting provided at desks

___ Each incandescent lamp and foot of incandescent strip used multiplied by 2, and each fluorescent and exit light multiplied by 1 should not add up to more than 50

(4 points)

Timed Design Exercise

Part 1 of 2

Part One of Design Exercise
River Keeper's Station, Full Version

Sheet

C-1

Scale   None

Student Control Number

TIMED DESIGN EXERCISE

Instructions to Students

1. Read all of these instructions before beginning the exercise.
2. Review the project and code requirements as well as the site plan P1-1.
3. Review the matrix, material options, and material schedules P1-1.
4. Review the interior elevation showing the window fenestration from the interior P1-1.
5. Review the floor plan P1-2.
6. Read the entire project description and carefully review the requirements in each area.
7. Complete the adjacency matrix P1-1.
8. Space plan on the sheet given to solve the problem defined (following).
9. Select finish materials for the floors and walls and indicate the best choice by circling it on the schedule P1-1.
10. Write your control number in the lower right of every sheet—even the ones that you don't write on.

Code Requirements

- All exterior doors are available for egress as they swing out and have a minimum clear opening of 3'.
- Egress paths of travel may not pass through areas that may be blocked, locked, or used for storage.
- Barrier free requires a 5' turning circle (show as a dotted line) at every change in direction. Paths of travel not required for egress are not bound by this restriction.
- Maintain a minimum width of 44" along accessible routes.
- Doors and storage units that open toward a path of travel may not limit the clear passage width when open.
- Doors to be a minimum of 3' clear width in all accessible spaces and a minimum 30" clear width otherwise.
- Doors in accessible areas must be flanked by clear wall space 18" on the pull side and 12" wide on the push side along the latching side.
- Sinks in barrier-free areas must have clear knee space below and may not encroach on the turning circle more than 6".
- Door swings may not encroach on turning circles.
- Habitable spaces in the living space/apartment must have an operable window.
- Floors in areas with sinks must be slip resistant.
- Surfaces in bathrooms and washrooms must be moisture resistant.

Design Requirements

All items, adjacencies, and attributes mentioned in this document are required in your passing solution. Use a freehand sketch or drafting to represent items in accurate scale. Draw your solution on drawing sheets provided using ink or felt tip (it will be assumed that all pencil is preliminary to your final solution and not intended as part of your final solution). You need only erase pencil marks that will interfere with comprehension of your solution.

Complete the partition and furniture plan on P1-1 showing typical required details (door swings, backs on chairs, pillows on bed, etc.) to the extent necessary to distinguish one type of item from another. Label all spaces listed in the project description. Include the lineal feet or cubic feet of storage required with the label for such items where the specific requirement is noted on the project requirements list.

Project Description

This river keeper's cabin is a research facility and meeting place; it is inhabited for a few months at a time throughout the year by grad students. This facility also provides overnight accommodations for visiting researchers studying ecosystems and wildlife. Views are important to all spaces.

All floor drains to sewer should be within a 36' diameter circle (circle location to be determined by you and indicated on the plan with a dotted line). Wall-mounted sinks and toilets may be an additional 8' outside circle, and chemical sink to reservoir in lab may be outside the circle.

Requirements for each functional area follow. Address the items to be represented as well as adjacencies and privacy considerations. Functions may be combined as long as all requirements are met.

With the exception of the front door, windows and doors can be located for best views and egress for your plan. You must determine the location and show these windows and the riverside door on your plan. Remember, bedroom windows are egress in case of fire.

Research, Investigative, and Facility Function

Lab

1. Two stations equipped as follows:
   a. Lab counter providing 12 lineal feet of counter space 30" deep
   b. Sink 12" wide × 18" from front to back; counter to be additional to work space
   c. Storage below to be accessible from work area
2. Desk providing 12 square feet of surface holds a computer and a phone, a task chair is to be provided
3. Sink 30" wide × 20" deep from front to back for dumping chemicals must be connected to a reservoir that is 15" tall × 24" wide and 15" deep from front to back
4. Locked cabinet for chemicals and supplies is 30" wide × 18" deep from front to back

Research and Records

1. Two desks each providing 12 square feet of work surface that holds a computer and phone. Each with a task chair.
2. 24" of lateral files
3. 25 lineal feet of bookshelves
4. Lounge chair and ottoman adjacent to a table that is 18" × 24" and a floor-standing task lamp

River Supplies

1. Closet 4' wide × 2' deep full height (for waders, raincoats, nets, etc.)
2. Bench 5' wide × 1.5' deep from front to back
3. Locked cabinet for boathouse and boat keys to be wall-mounted; 10" × 10" × 4" deep from front to back
4. Drip tray with drain 24" × 24" with hang rod above

This area is to be located near an entrance that you must indicate with a door on the riverside of the building.

Utility Room

120 square feet centrally located; must be within the plumbing circle defined by dotted line on solution sheet.

Classroom

1. 20 chairs with attached, flip-up writing surface, each measuring approximately 18" wide × 24" deep from front to back
2. Folding table for presenter/instructor is 30" × 60" with 3 chairs
3. Projector indicated by dotted line on floor plan is 10" × 10" mounted 8' from screen
4. Projection screen mounted to wall is 5' wide
5. Closet 30" deep from front to back × 5' wide, full height

Classroom must be barrier-free.

Living Space for Staff and Visitors

Guest coats must be stored immediately adjacent to a door from the outside.

Sitting Room

1. Lounge seating for four to six
2. Set-down surface reachable from each seat
3. Shelving unit containing TV 30" wide × 24" deep × 28" tall; stacked stereo equipment requires 18" wide × 17" deep × 15" tall space when stacked
4. 40 lineal feet of book shelving

Kitchen

1. 15 lineal feet clear counter space over base cabinets and appliances
2. 10 lineal feet of upper cabinets
3. Full-height refrigerator 30" wide × 28" deep
4. Undercounter dishwasher 24" × 24"
5. Microwave 21" wide × 18" deep × 15" tall
6. Sink 24" wide × 18" deep from front to back
7. Range 24" wide × 30" deep
8. Table and chairs for 6 people

Two sleep spaces for grad students to contain:

1. Double bed 54" wide × 75" long
2. Set-down surface each side of bed minimum 24" wide × 20" deep
3. Dresser 6' wide × 20" deep from front to back × 30" tall
4. Closet with 3' of long hanging and 4' of short/double hanging

Bathroom for each grad student immediately adjacent to sleep spaces

1. Vanity cabinet 30" wide × 22" deep containing sink
2. Toilet
3. Tub 2'5" wide × 5'0" long with shower. Indicate location of fittings (shower head and faucet)
4. Linen closet 24" wide × 24" deep full height

Two sleep spaces for visitors to contain:

1. Double bed 54" wide × 75" long
2. Pair of nightstands 24" wide × 20" deep × 26" tall, with drawer storage
3. Closet with 1.5 lineal feet of hanging
4. Luggage rack 2' wide × 18" deep from front to back

One of these rooms must be barrier free.

Bathroom to be shared by visitors

1. Vanity cabinet 30" wide × 22" deep containing sink
2. Toilet
3. Shower 42" wide and 36" deep

The toilet and sink in this bath must be accessible to all guests for use as powder room in addition to overnight guests. This bathroom to be barrier free for toilet and sink.

Timed Design Exercise

Part 1 of 2

Site Plan
Elevation
Matrix
Schedule
River Keeper's Station, Full Version

Sheet **P1-1**

Scale 1/8" = 1'-0"

Control Number

Adjacency Matrix

Use only these symbols; do not make up your own symbols.

● Direct Adjacency
○ Convenient Adjacency
X Remote

	Main Entry	Lab	Research	Classroom	River Supplies	Utilities	Sitting Rm	Kitchen	Grad Suite	Guest Rm	Guest Bath
Main Entry											
Lab											
Research											
Classroom											
River Supplies											
Utilities											
Sitting Rm											
Kitchen											
Grad Suite											
Guest Rm											
Guest Bath											

F	Floor
F1	45 oz low-level loop commercial nylon carpet
F2	Stained concrete sealed 3 coats matte nonslip urethane
F3	Ungauged slate with heavy cleft face acrylic high-gloss sealer
F4	Recycled rubber tiles
W	Walls
W1	Washable semigloss, low VOC paint
W2	Washable satin, low VOC paint
W3	Ceramic tile
W4	Textured commercial vinyl wall covering

Circle the most appropriate choice from those listed to the right by referencing the table above for material descriptions.

Area	Floor			Walls		
Class Rm	F1	F2	F3	W1	W3	W4
Lab	F3	F2	F1	W1	W2	W3
Guest BR	F3	F4	F1	W1	W3	W4
Kitchen	F1	F2	F4	W1	W2	W4

N

Ⓐ **Site Plan**

Ⓑ **Exterior Elevation**
Scale 1/8" = 1'-0"

River Keeper's Station, Full Version | **Timed Design Exercises** | Part 1 of 2 (CD)

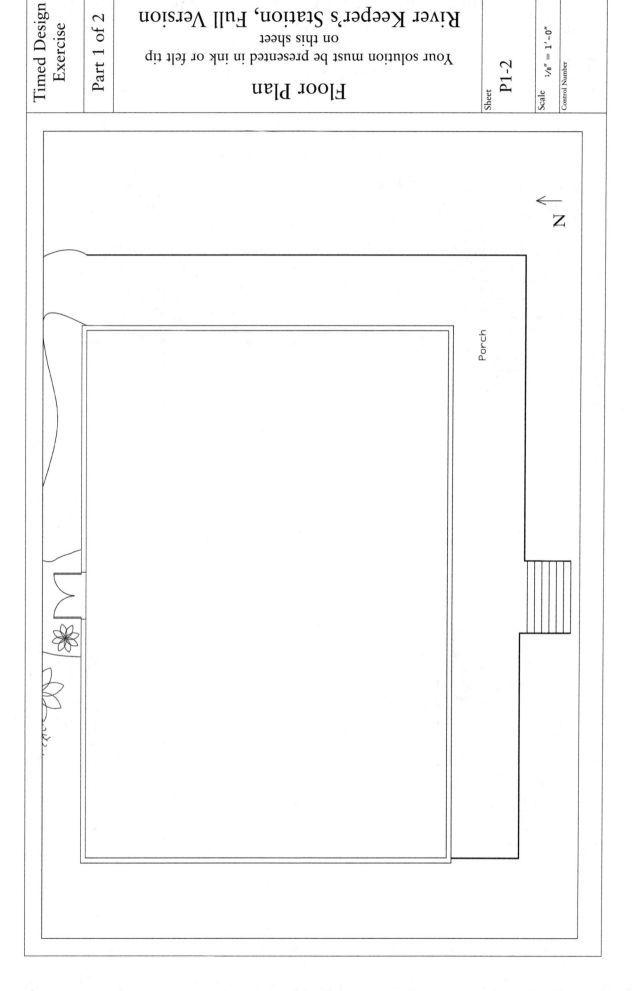

Timed Design Exercise		
Part 1 of 2		

River Keeper's Station, Full Version

Your solution must be presented in ink or felt tip on this sheet

Floor Plan

Sheet	**P1-2**
Scale	1/8" = 1'-0"
Control Number	

Porch

N

Part Two of Design Exercise
River Keeper's Station, Full Version

Sheet

C-2

Scale None

Student Control Number

TIMED DESIGN EXERCISE

Instructions to Students

1. Read all of these instructions before beginning the exercise.
2. Review the project and code requirements and additional scope of services.
3. Review the floor plan P2-1; notice the layout for your lighting and electrical planning and also the elevation symbols indicating the two elevations for the reception desk, which are to be drawn on sheet P2-1 at 1/4" = 1'-0" (requirements follow).
4. Review all of the symbols and electrical requirements on sheet P2-2.
5. Locate the electrical and communication devices required on the electrical/data/phone plan, sheet P2-2.
6. Create a reflected ceiling plan on sheet P2-3 showing all lighting locations.
7. Draw required circuitry and switching locations for a functional design.
8. Write your control number where indicated in the lower right corner of every sheet—even the ones that you don't write on.
9. Select the best choice from the equipment listed in the legends and use only that equipment and those symbols. Do not add equipment or make up your own symbols.

Code Requirements

- All electrical outlets must be located 18" AFF unless noted otherwise.
- Exit signage must be visible upon exiting all enclosed spaces and positioned to direct people safely out of the building without confusion as to the exit locations. Exit signs must not direct people into the enclosed space of another room before delivering them to an exit to the outdoors.
- Where practical, wall outlets and ports are preferred over floor-mounted outlets and ports.
- Electricity, voice, and data devices required of the reception desk are to be brought up into and permanently affixed within the built-in reception desk.
- Electricity, voice, and data devices for sales offices will not be brought up into the portable desks and must be configured so no cords span open space where a person might walk.

Additional Scope of Services

The game warden is a separate function from the river keeper, but the two departments do collaborate, as they have overlapping missions. It is a goal of this state that the warden's offices be viewed by citizens as an outdoorsman's resource rather than a policing function, and an institutional atmosphere is to be avoided as much as possible.

Design Requirements

All items, adjacencies, and attributes mentioned in this document are required in your solution. Use a freehand sketch or drafting to represent items in accurate scale. Draw your solution on drawing sheets provided using ink or felt tip (it will be assumed that all pencil is preliminary to your final solution and not intended as part of your final solution).

Project Description

Reception Desk

1. The design of the reception desk is to be congruent with nature themes.
2. A computer monitor sits on the desk 30" AFF. The device that connects and powers the cpu is to be located 24" AFF in a closed-door storage unit within the desk.
3. A phone is also located on the desk connected and powered by a device located in the vertical support for the transaction top.
4. A printer is located on a pullout shelf below desk height.
5. Two trash containers (one for paper, one for trash) are each 8" × 12" × 15" tall.
6. A box file pedestal base for supplies and filing for current projects.
7. Additional closed storage with one adjustable shelf for paper storage.
8. Label all finishes/surface materials for the desk; note incremental and overall dimensions.
9. Use hidden lines and notes for all requirements that are not visible from assigned views.

Electrical Plan

1. Review the requirements on sheet P2-2 and provide for all required devices.
2. Note heights of all devices that are not to be located at the standard 18" AFF.

Lighting/Reflected Ceiling Plan

1. Energy conservation to be balanced with effective lighting techniques in display and sales areas.
2. Solution to be safe and conform with codes.

Timed Design Exercise

Part 2 of 2

Floor Plan
River Keeper's Station, Full Version

Sheet **P2-1**

Scale 1/8" = 1'-0"

Control Number

Use the space below to draw (to scale) your design for the reception desk showing all equipment devices, dimensions, and material descriptions.

Locked Storage

Restroom

Files

Coats

Warden's Office

Files

Warden's Offices

Reception Desk

Supplies

Community Meeting

Conference Room

A

B

Files

A Elevation of Customer Side of Reception Desk
Scale: 1/4" = 1'-0"

B Elevation of Staff Side of Reception Desk
Scale: 1/4" = 1'-0"

Electrical/Data/Phone Plan
River Keeper's Station, Full Version

Sheet **P2-2**

Scale 1/8" = 1'-0"

Control Number

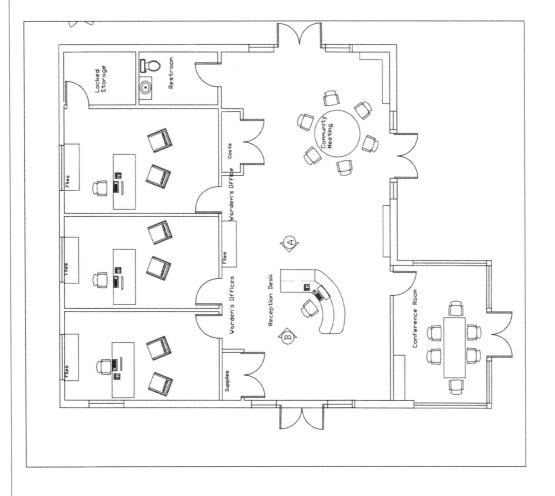

Electrical Legend

Symbol	Description
	Duplex outlet
GFI	Ground Fault Interrupt duplex outlet
	Quadruplex outlet
	220-volt outlet
	Cat 3 phone port
	Cat 5 data port
	Voice and data port
	Voice/data/power
	Floor duplex outlet
	Floor phone port
	Floor data port

Use only these symbols to communicate your design. Do not make up your own symbols.

Equipment List   Note all heights that deviate from typical 18" AFF

Qty	Location and requirements
1	Reception desk: phone/data/power in desktop
1	Reception desk: one duplex outlet at transaction counter
1	Reception desk: one phone line 24" AFF for computer
1	One duplex 30" credenza in conference room
2	Voice/data/power in floor under conference table
1	Each warden desk: duplex each office
1	Each warden desk: phone/data/power each office
1	Each warden desk: phone each office
1	Duplex in supplies cabinet for DustBuster
1	Duplex in floor under community meeting table
1	Wall outlet for decorative clock above receptionist files

Refer to this list as you prepare your electrical/data/power plan; select and show only these items on that plan.

Timed Design Exercise

Part 2 of 2

Reflected Ceiling Plan
River Keeper's Station, Full Version

Sheet P2-3

Scale ⅛" = 1'-0"

Control Number

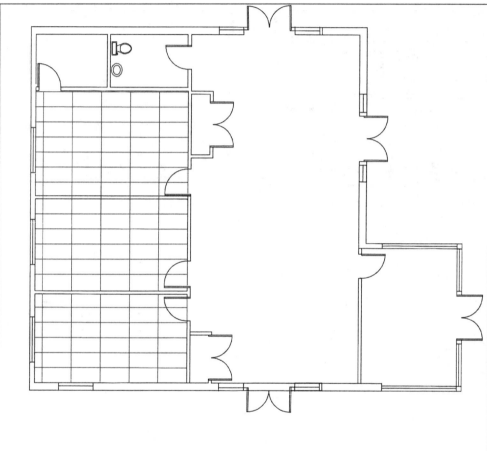

Lighting Legend

Wall	Ceiling	
	®	Recessed incandescent
®LV	®LV	Recessed incandescent low voltage
®CFL	®CFL	Recessed compact fluorescent
	▱	Recessed fluorescent troffer
– – –		Hidden light fixture fluorescent T5 or xenon strip light
	⊗	Portable task or table lamp
	▽—	Track lighting—broad side of triangle indicates beam side
®E	®E	Security lighting with backup battery power (always on)
⊗	⊗	Exit sign (dark portion indicates location of lettering)
	▣	Exhaust fan/light
$		Light switch
$₃		3–pole switch
$D		Dimmer switch

Refer to this list as you prepare your Lighting Plan; show only these items on your plan; use only these fixtures to solve the problem and use only these symbols—do not make up your own symbols.

DESIGN SCENARIO 4

River Keeper's Station,
Lite Version

RIVER KEEPER'S STATION

Lite Version (119.5 points total)

Suggested Scoring Part One

The following *must* be met for 5 points:

___ Living functions are not intermingled with business functions.

___ Private living areas are to be visually screened.

___ Safe egress is available to both functional spaces.

(15 points)

The following *must* be met for 2 points each (code requirements listed on C-1 and info on P1-1):

___ Egress is not blocked, locked, or used for storage.

___ Paths of egress are barrier free and minimum of 44 inches wide.

___ Safe and quick egress is provided from sleeping areas.

___ Doors along paths of exit travel are 36 inches wide and do not impinge upon clear 44-inch-wide path.

___ Open storage does not impinge on 44-inch-wide clear paths of exit travel.

___ Doors that are not along an exit path of travel nor in handicapped-accessible spaces have at least 30 inches clear open width.

___ Accessible doors have 18 inches clear wall space on the pull side of the latch edge and 12 inches on the pull side of the hinge edge and have a clear width of 32 inches.

___ Door swings do not encroach on turning circles.

___ Habitable spaces have natural light and ventilation.

___ Access to business functions can be gained without extensive travel through living space.

___ All drains fall within a 36-ft-diameter circle, which is shown on the plan as a dotted line.

___ Windows and doors are shown correctly.

___ Consideration of rhythm of fenestration is evident in window placement.

___ Solution is correctly portrayed entirely on sheet P1-2.

___ Configuration and furnishings are located to maximize views.

(30 points)

The following *should* be on matrix and plan for 1 point each:

___ Direct adjacency BRs to Baths

___ Direct adjacency Kitchen to Dining

___ Convenient adjacency Powder Room to Meeting Room

___ Convenient adjacency Entrance to Living Room

___ Convenient adjacency Living Room to Powder Room

___ Convenient adjacency Entrance to Meeting Room

___ Material schedule
Classroom floor F-4 walls W-4
Lab floor F-2 walls W-1
Guest BR floor F-1 walls W-4
Kitchen floor F-4 walls W-1

(7 points)

The following *should* be met for 1/2 point each (each requirement listed per space on C-1):

Lab

___ Desk with 12 SF of surface with chair

___ Cabinet 30 inches wide x 18 inches deep noted locked for chemicals

___ Lab station to contain:
12 LF counter 30 inches deep
Sink 12 inches × 18 inches
Storage below counter accessible

Research and Records

___ Two desks with 12 SF of surface and two executive chairs

___ 24 feet of lateral files

___ 25 lineal feet of book shelves

River Supplies

___ Closet 4 feet wide and 2 feet deep with hang rod

___ Bench 5 feet x 1.5 feet front to back

___ Door located on river side of this room ___

Utility Room

____ 120 SF shown within plumbing circle

Classroom

____ 15 chairs with flip-up writing surface

____ Folding table for presenter 30 inches × 60 inches with three chairs

____ Closet 30 inches deep from front to back and 5 feet wide

____ Barrier free

Front Entrance

____ Guest coats 6 feet of hang rod or 12 feet of hooks

Living Room

____ Lounge seating for six

____ Set-down surface at each seat

____ Shelving unit for TV and stereo minimum 30 inches wide × 24 inches deep from front to back

____ 20 lineal feet of book shelves

Kitchen

____ 15 LF of base and 10 LF of uppers

____ Refrigerator 30 inches × 28 inches × 72 inches tall

____ Dishwasher 2 feet × 2 feet

____ Microwave 21 inches wide × 18 inches deep

____ Sink 24 inches x 18 inches

____ Range 24 inches wide × 30 inches deep

____ Table and seating for six

Grad Student Sleep Spaces

____ Two such spaces

____ Double bed (54 inches × 75 inches) with minimum 2 feet clearance on each side

____ Set-down surface on each side, minimum 24 inches wide × 20 inches deep

____ Dresser 6 feet wide × 20 inches deep

____ Closet 3 LF of long hanging and 4 LF of short hanging

____ One room to be barrier free

____ Accommodates one sleepover guest

Grad Student Shared Bath

____ Vanity 30 inches wide × 22 inches deep with one sink

____ Toilet and tub (2.5 feet × 5 feet) shower fittings noted

____ Linen closet 2 feet × 2 feet full height

Powder Room

____ Toilet with grab bars shown

____ Sink

____ Barrier free

(19½ points)

One point awarded for each of the following:

____ No item of furniture taller than 3 feet should be placed in front of windows

____ All required items are illustrated or labeled to differentiate from other item types

____ Flow and logic prevail over choppy and cluttered layout

(3 points)

Suggested Scoring Part Two

These requirements *should* be met for 2 points each (overall quality issues):

____ Plans are completed using only the selections and symbols given

____ Outlets are noted at 18 inches AFF Typ. except where instructed otherwise

____ Exit signage positioned for visibility from all locations (except inside washroom)

____ Outlets are wall outlets wherever practical

(8 points)

Reception Desk Elevations

These requirements *should* be met for 2 points each:

____ The desk is accurately sketched or drafted to scale as required by elevation markers

____ Materials noted are congruent with nature themes

____ Desk height at computer 30 inches

____ Phone jack in vertical support for transaction surface

____ Printer on pull out shelf below desktop

___ Two trash containers 8 inches $\times$ 12 inches $\times$ 15 inches tall

___ Box/file pedestal

___ Closed storage for paper

___ Dotted lines show locations of required elements not shown by views assigned

(18 points)

Electrical Plan

The following *should* be met for 1 point each:

Reception Desk

___ Voice/data/power

___ Phone

___ Duplex 24 inches AFF

Conference Room

___ Voice/data/power under conference table

Warden Desk

___ Voice/data/power in wall convenient to desk

___ Duplex in wall convenient to desk

___ Phone jack in wall convenient to desk

(7 points)

Lighting Plan

The following *should* be met for 1 point each:

___ Fluorescent lights for ambient light

___ Flexible track for performance lighting

___ Exit signage visible from all locations in shop (outside of restroom)

___ Minimum two light fixtures in conference room

___ Minimum five light fixtures in reception/community table room

___ Minimum two light fixtures in each office

___ Minimum one light fixture in washroom

___ Minimum one light fixture in locked storage

(8 points)

The following *should* be met for 1 point each:

___ Fan/light in bathroom

___ Emergency lighting incorporated into scheme

___ Task lighting provided at desks

___ Each incandescent lamp and foot of incandescent strip multiplied by 2 and each fluorescent and exit light multiplied by 1 should not add up to more than 50

(4 points)

TIMED DESIGN EXERCISE

Instructions to Students

1. Read all of these instructions before beginning the exercise.
2. Review the project and code requirements as well as the site plan P1-1.
3. Review the matrix, material options, and material schedules P1-1.
4. Review the interior elevation showing the window fenestration from the interior P1-1.
5. Review the floor plan P1-2.
6. Read the entire project description and carefully review the requirements in each area.
7. Complete the adjacency matrix P1-1.
8. Space plan on the sheet given to solve the problem defined (following).
9. Select finish materials for the floors and walls and indicate the best choice by circling it on the schedule P1-1.
10. Write your control number in the lower right of every sheet—even the ones that you don't write on.

Code Requirements

- All exterior doors are available for egress as they swing out and have a minimum clear opening of 3'.
- Egress paths of travel may not pass through areas that may be blocked, locked, or used for storage.
- Barrier free requires a 5' turning circle (show as a dotted line) at every change in direction. Paths of travel not required for egress are not bound by this restriction.
- Maintain a minimum width of 44" along accessible routes.
- Doors and storage units that open toward a path of travel may not limit the clear passage width when open.
- Doors to be a minimum of 3' clear width in all accessible spaces and a minimum 30" clear width otherwise.
- Doors in accessible areas must be flanked by clear wall space 18" on the pull side and 12" wide on the push side along the latching side.
- Sinks in barrier-free areas must have clear knee space below and may not encroach on the turning circle more than 6"
- Door swings may not encroach on turning circles.
- Habitable spaces in the living space/apartment must have an operable window.
- Floors in areas with sinks must be slip resistant.
- Surfaces in bathrooms and washrooms must be moisture resistant.

Design Requirements

All items, adjacencies, and attributes mentioned in this document are required in your passing solution. Use a freehand sketch or drafting to represent items in accurate scale. Draw your solution on drawing sheets provided using ink or felt tip (it will be assumed that all pencil is preliminary to your final solution and not intended as part of your final solution). You need only erase pencil marks that will interfere with comprehension of your solution.

Complete the partition and furniture plan on P1-1, showing typical required details (door swings, backs on chairs, pillows on bed, etc.) to the extent necessary to distinguish one type of item from another. Label all spaces listed in the project description. Include the lineal feet or cubic feet of storage required with the label for such items where the specific requirement is noted on the project requirements list.

Project Description

This river keeper's cabin is a research facility and meeting place; it is inhabited for a few months at a time throughout the year by grad students. This facility also provides overnight accommodations for visiting researchers studying ecosystems and wildlife. Views are important to all spaces.

All floor drains to sewer should be within a 36' diameter circle (circle location to be determined by you and indicated on the plan with a dotted line). Wall-mounted sinks and toilets may be an additional 8' outside circle and chemical sink to reservoir in lab may be outside the circle.

Requirements for each functional area follow. Address the items to be represented as well as adjacencies and privacy considerations. Functions may be combined as long as all requirements are met.

With the exception of the front door, windows and doors can be located for best views and egress for your plan. You must determine and show these locations on your plan.

Research, Investigative, and Facility Function

Lab

1. Station equipped as follows:
   a. Lab counter providing 12 lineal feet of counter space 30" deep
   b. Sink 12" wide × 18" from front to back; counter to be additional to work space
   c. Storage below to be accessible from work area
2. Desk providing 12 square feet of surface holds a computer and a phone, a task chair is to be provided.
3. Locked cabinet for chemicals and supplies is 30" wide × 18" deep from front to back.

Research and Records

1. Two desks each providing 12 square feet of work surface that holds a computer and phone. Each with a task chair.
2. 24' of lateral files
3. 25 lineal feet of bookshelves

River Supplies

1. Closet 4' wide × 2' deep full height (for waders, raincoats, nets, etc.)
2. Bench 5' wide × 1.5' deep from front to back
This area is to be located near an entrance on the riverside of the building

Utility Room

120 square feet centrally located; must be within the plumbing circle defined by dotted line on solution sheet.

Classroom

1. 15 chairs, each measuring approximately 18" wide × 24" deep from front to back
2. Folding table for presenter/instructor is 30" × 60" with 3 chairs
3. Closet 30" deep from front to back × 5' wide, full height
Classroom must be barrier-free.

Living Space for Staff and Visitors

Guest coats for 26 must be stored immediately adjacent to a door from the outside. Allocate 6' of closet or 12" of wall for staggered high/low pegs.

Sitting Room

1. Lounge seating for four to six
2. Set-down surface reachable from each seat
3. Shelving unit containing TV 30" wide × 24" deep × 28" tall; stacked stereo equipment requires 18" wide × 17" deep × 15" tall space when stacked
4. 20 lineal feet of book shelving

Kitchen

1. 15 lineal feet clear counter space over base cabinets and appliances
2. 10 lineal feet of upper cabinets
3. Full-height refrigerator 30" wide × 28" deep
4. Undercounter dishwasher 24" × 24"
5. Microwave 21" wide × 18" deep × 15" tall
6. Sink 24" wide × 18" deep from front to back
7. Range 24" wide × 30" deep
8. Table and chairs for 6 people

Two separate sleep spaces for grad students to contain:
1. Double bed 54" wide × 75" long
2. Set-down surface each side of bed minimum 24" wide × 20" deep
3. Dresser 6' wide × 20" deep from front to back × 30" tall
4. Closet with 3' of long hanging and 4' of short/double hanging

Shared bathroom immediately adjacent to sleep spaces
1. Vanity cabinet 30" wide × 22" deep containing sink
2. Toilet
3. Tub 2'5" wide × 5'0" long with shower. Indicate location of fittings (shower head and faucet)
4. Linen closet 24" wide × 24" deep full height

Bathroom to be used by visitors
1. Vanity cabinet 24" wide × 22" deep containing sink
2. Toilet
This bath must be accessible.

Timed Design Exercise

Part 1 of 2

Part One of Design Exercise
River Keeper's Station, Lite Version

Sheet

C-1

Scale   None

Student Control Number

Timed Design Exercise

Part 1 of 2

Site Plan
Elevation
Matrix
Schedule
River Keeper's Station, Lite Version

Sheet P1-1

Scale None

Control Number

Adjacency Matrix

Use only these symbols; do not make up your own symbols.

● Direct Adjacency
○ Convenient Adjacency
X Remote

	Main Entry	Lab	Research	Classroom	River Supplies	Utilities	Sitting Rm	Kitchen	Grad Suite	Grad Bath	Guest Bath
Main Entry											
Lab											
Research											
Classroom											
River Supplies											
Utilities											
Sitting Rm											
Kitchen											
Grad Rms											
Grad Bath											
Guest Bath											

F	Floor
F1	45 oz low-level loop commercial nylon carpet
F2	Stained concrete sealed 3 coats matte nonslip urethane
F3	Ungauged slate with heavy cleft face acrylic high-gloss sealer
F4	Recycled rubber tiles
W	Walls
W1	Washable gloss low VOC paint
W2	Satin, low VOC paint
W3	Ceramic tile
W4	Textured commercial vinyl wall covering

Circle the most appropriate choice from those listed to the right by referencing the table above for material descriptions.

Area	Floor				Walls			
Class Rm	F1	F2	F3		W1	W2	W3	W4
Lab	F1	F2	F3		W1	W2	W3	W4
Sleep Space	F1	F4	F3		W1	W3	W4	
Kitchen	F1	F3	F4		W1	W2	W3	W4

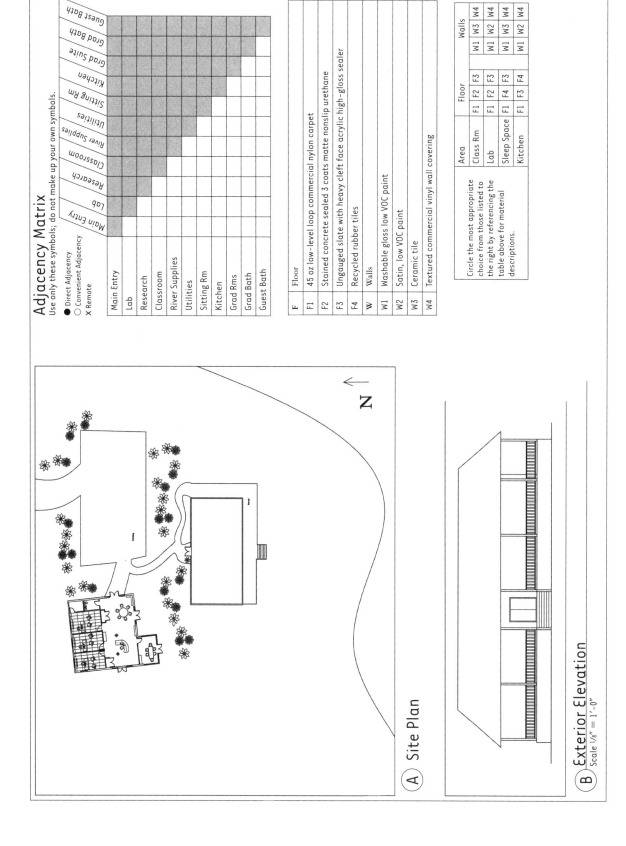

N

(A) Site Plan

(B) Exterior Elevation
Scale 1/8" = 1'-0"

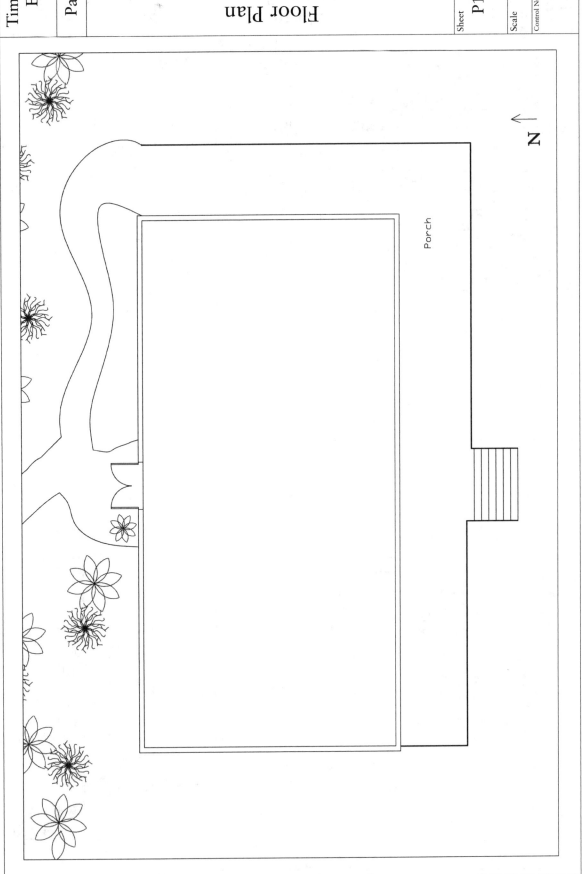

Porch

N

Floor Plan

Your solution must be presented in ink or felt tip on this sheet

River Keeper's Station, Lite Version

Timed Design Exercise

Part 1 of 2

Sheet P1-2

Scale ⅛" = 1'-0"

Control Number

Part Two of Design Exercise
River Keeper's Station, Lite Version

TIMED DESIGN EXERCISE

Instructions to Students

1. Read all of these instructions before beginning the exercise.
2. Review the project and code requirements and additional scope of services.
3. Review the floor plan P2-1; notice the layout for your lighting and electrical planning and also the elevation symbols indicating the two elevations for the reception desk, which are to be drawn on sheet P2-1 at 1/4" = 1'-0" (requirements follow).
4. Review all of the symbols and electrical requirements on sheet P2-2.
5. Locate the electrical and communication devices required on the electrical/data/phone plan, sheet P2-2.
6. Create a reflected ceiling plan on sheet P2-3 showing all lighting locations.
7. Draw required circuitry and switching locations for a functional design.
8. Write your control number where indicated in the lower right corner of every sheet—even the ones that you don't write on.
9. Select the best choice from the equipment listed in the legends and use only that equipment and those symbols. Do not add equipment or make up your own symbols.

Code Requirements

- All electrical outlets must be located 18" AFF unless noted otherwise.
- Exit signage must be visible upon exiting all enclosed spaces and positioned to direct people safely out of the building without confusion as to the exit locations. Exit signs must not direct people into the enclosed space of another room before delivering them to an exit to the outdoors.
- Where practical, wall outlets and ports are preferred over floor-mounted outlets and ports.
- Electricity, voice, and data devices required of the reception desk are to be brought up into and permanently affixed within the built-in reception desk.
- Electricity, voice, and data devices for sales offices will not be brought up into the portable desks and must be configured so no cords span open space where a person might walk.

Additional Scope of Services

The game warden is a separate function from the river keeper, but the two departments do collaborate, as they have overlapping missions. It is a goal of this state that the warden's offices be viewed by citizens as an outdoorsman's resource rather than a policing function, and an institutional atmosphere is to be avoided as much as possible.

Design Requirements

All items, adjacencies, and attributes mentioned in this document are required in your solution. Use a freehand sketch or drafting to represent items in accurate scale. Draw your solution on drawing sheets provided using ink or felt tip (it will be assumed that all pencil is preliminary to your final solution and not intended as part of your final solution).

Show your design for the reception desk with elevations where indicated on P2-1.

Reception Desk

1. The design of the reception desk is to be congruent with nature themes.
2. A computer monitor sits on the desk 30" AFF. The device that connects and powers the cpu is to be located 24" AFF in a closed-door storage unit within the desk.
3. A phone is also located on the desk connected and powered by a device located in the vertical support for the transaction top.
4. A printer is located on a pullout shelf below desk height.
5. Two trash containers (one for paper, one for trash) are each 8" × 12" × 15" tall.
6. A box file pedestal base for supplies and filing for current projects.
7. Additional closed storage with one adjustable shelf for paper storage.
8. Label all finishes/surface materials for the desk; note incremental and overall dimensions.
9. Use hidden lines and notes for all requirements that are not visible from assigned views.

Electrical Plan

1. Review the requirements on sheet P2-2 and provide for all required devices.
2. Note heights of all devices that are not to be located at the standard 18" AFF.

Lighting/Reflected Ceiling Plan

1. Energy conservation to be balanced with effective lighting techniques in display and sales areas.
2. Solution to be safe and conform with codes.

Timed Design Exercise

Part 2 of 2

Floor Plan
River Keeper's Station, Lite Version

Sheet P2-1

Scale 1/8" = 1'-0"

Control Number

Use the space below to draw (to scale) your design for the reception desk showing all equipment devices, dimensions, and material descriptions.

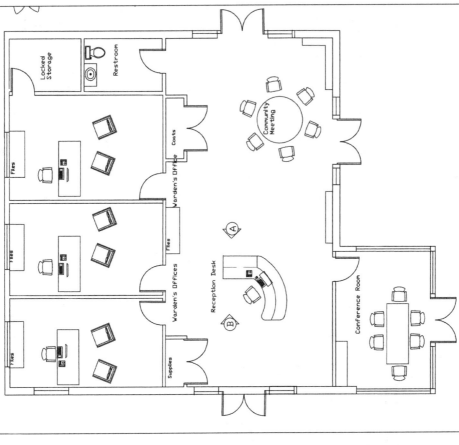

A Elevation of Customer Side of Reception Desk
Scale: 1/4" = 1'-0"

B Elevation of Staff Side of Reception Desk
Scale: 1/4" = 1'-0"

Electrical/Data/Phone Plan
River Keeper's Station, Lite Version

Sheet P2-2

Scale 1/8" = 1'-0"

Control Number

Electrical Legend

	Duplex outlet
GFI	Ground Fault Interrupt duplex outlet
	Quadruplex outlet
	220-volt outlet
	Cat 3 phone port
	Cat 5 data port
	Voice and data port
	Voice/data/power
	Floor duplex outlet
	Floor phone port
	Floor data port

Use only these symbols to communicate your design. Do not make up your own symbols.

Equipment List Note all heights that deviate from typical 18" AFF

Qty	Location and requirements
1	Reception desk: phone/data/power in desktop
1	Reception desk: one phone line 24" AFF for computer
1	Voice/data/power in floor under conference table
1	Each warden desk: duplex each office
1	Each warden desk: phone/data/power each office
1	Each warden desk: phone each office

Refer to this list as you prepare your electrical/data/power plan; select and show only these items on that plan.

River Keeper's Station, Lite Version   Timed Design Exercises   Part 2 of 2   CD

Timed Design Exercise

Part 2 of 2

Reflected Ceiling Plan
River Keeper's Station, Lite Version

Sheet P2-3

Scale 1/8" = 1'-0"

Control Number

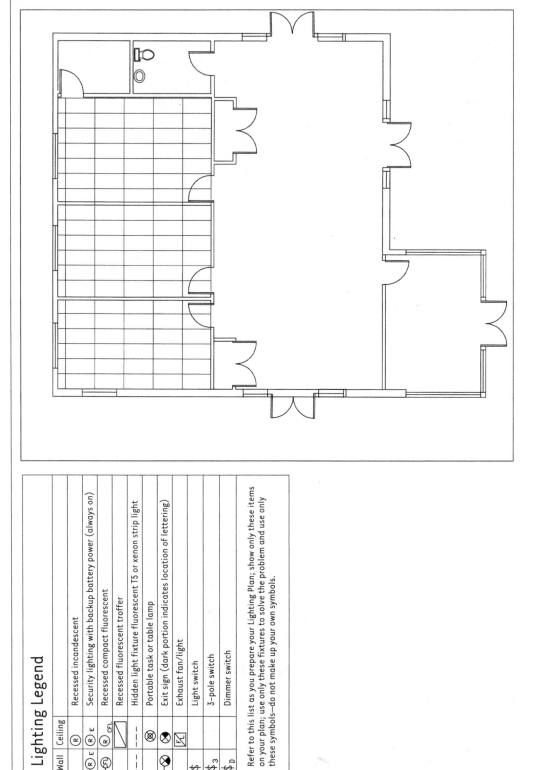

Lighting Legend

Wall	Ceiling	
	®	Recessed incandescent
⊢®ᴇ	®ᴇ	Security lighting with backup battery power (always on)
⊢©ꜰʟ	®ᴄꜰʟ	Recessed compact fluorescent
	▱	Recessed fluorescent troffer
— — —	— — —	Hidden light fixture fluorescent T5 or xenon strip light
	⊗	Portable task or table lamp
	⊗	Exit sign (dark portion indicates location of lettering)
	⊠	Exhaust fan/light
$		Light switch
$₃		3-pole switch
$ᴅ		Dimmer switch

Refer to this list as you prepare your Lighting Plan; show only these items on your plan; use only these fixtures to solve the problem and use only these symbols—do not make up your own symbols.